Our World

SECOND EDITION

COMBO 4B SPLIT

Series Editors
Joan Kang Shin and
JoAnn (Jodi) Crandall

Student's Book Authors
Kate Cory-Wright
Sue Harmes

NATIONAL GEOGRAPHIC LEARNING

Australia · Brazil · Mexico · Singapore · United Kingdom · United States

OUR WORLD

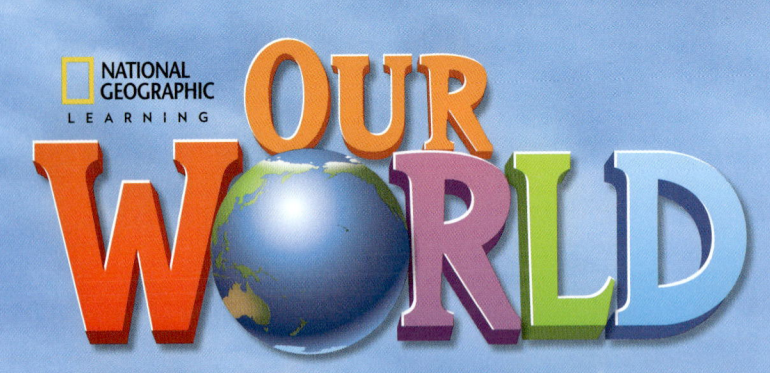

TR: 10.1

This is our world.
Everybody's got a song to sing.
Each boy and girl.
This is our world!
I say, "Our." You say, "World."
Our!
World!
Our!
World!
I say, "Boy." You say, "Girl."
Boy!
Girl!

Boy!
Girl!
I say, "Everybody move!"
I say, "Everybody stop!"
Everybody, stop!
This is our world.
Everybody's got a song to sing.
Each boy and girl.
This is our world!

Student's Book

Unit 6 Wonders of the Sea.. 4
Unit 7 Good Idea!... 20
Unit 8 That's Really Interesting!.................................. 36
Unit 9 The Science of Fun.. 52
Units 4-6 Extended Reading: Oceans of Plastic...................... 68
Units 7-9 Extended Reading: Leonardo da Vinci...................... 70

Units 1-3 Let's Talk

Let's Talk   Hello!... 72
             I agree!... 73

Units 4-6 Let's Talk

Let's Talk   What's wrong?.. 74
             I don't understand....................................... 75

Units 7-9 Let's Talk

Let's Talk   Wow, that's cool!.. 76
             What does that mean?..................................... 77

Workbook

Unit 6 Wonders of the Sea.. 78
Unit 7 Good Idea!.. 90
Unit 8 That's Really Interesting!................................. 102
Unit 9 The Science of Fun... 114
Activities and Games.. 127

Student's Book
Cutouts... 131
Irregular Verbs... 139
Stickers

Unit 6

Wonders of the Sea

In this unit, I will . . .
- name and describe sea life.
- talk about how we can protect the oceans.
- talk about future events.
- write to describe how things are different.

Check T for *True* and F for *False*.

1. The seal is underwater. T F
2. The seal is behind the seaweed. T F
3. Seaweed grows in the ocean. T F

4. Write a caption for this photo.
   _____

A harbor seal, California, USA

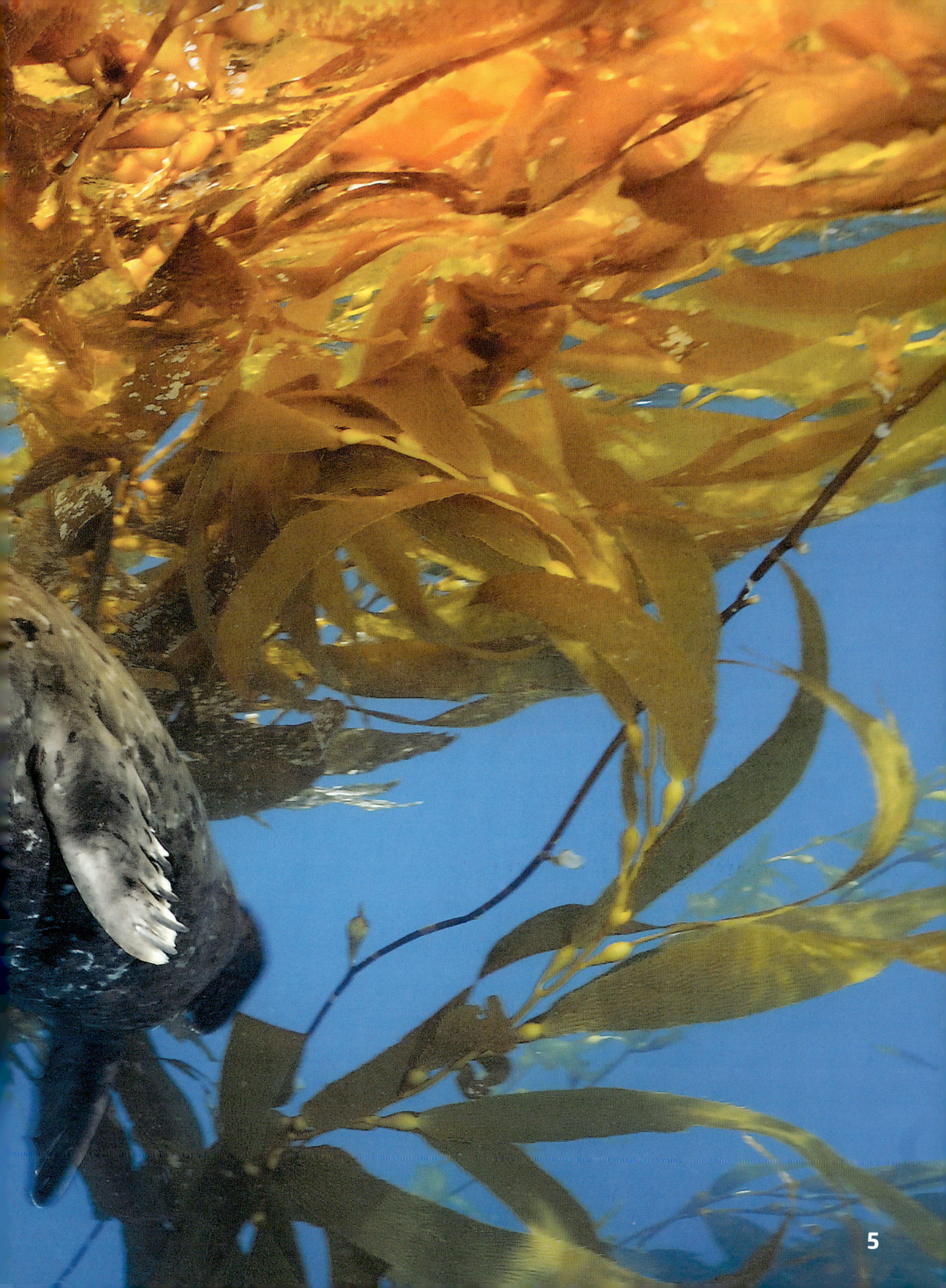

VOCABULARY 1

1 **Listen and read.** TR: 6.1

2 **Listen and repeat.** TR: 6.2

We use the oceans for fun, for transportation, and, more importantly, we use the oceans for food. We must stop **pollution**. We must protect the oceans or our **resources** will **disappear**.

The oceans are full of wonderful sea life. Most of the **creatures** we know stay near the top **layer** of the water, called the sunlit **zone**. In this zone, **sunlight** goes down to about 200 m (656 ft.).

a whale

The middle layer of the water is called the twilight zone. This is because there isn't much light. This zone goes down to about 1,000 m (3,300 ft.). Many different types of fish live in this layer. Some of them look very strange.

a squid

The mysterious bottom layer of water is almost completely black. The only light comes from the creatures who live here. It is called the **midnight** zone because sunlight doesn't reach below 1,000 m (3,300 ft.). Some amazing animals live in this deepest part of the ocean.

6 Unit 6

fish

a dolphin

a sea turtle

a shark

sea sponges

an octopus

3 **Ask and answer.** Work with a partner. What did you learn?

Where do squid live?

Most squid live in the twilight zone.

SONG

1 **Listen, read, and sing.** TR: 6.3

Protect the Seas

CHORUS
Please, please protect the seas.
Put good deeds into motion.
Help save the oceans.

We must protect
the wonders of the seas,
to make a better world
for you and me.

We must stop polluting
the ocean blue.
An octopus would like that,
and so would you.

CHORUS

We must protect
the wonders of the seas,
to make a better world
for you and me.

When we make a mess,
we can't dump it in the sea.
Sharks don't want that.
Do we?

There are layers in the ocean below.
There are creatures there that we don't know.
They live deep underwater. They don't breathe air,
but our world is a part of theirs.

CHORUS

2 **Ask and answer.** Work with a partner.

1. What are two common ways we pollute the oceans?
2. What are some ways we use the oceans?
3. Why is it important to care for the oceans?

Honshu, Japan

GRAMMAR 1

> **Have to, must, can't, and don't** TR: 6.4
> We **have to** keep the oceans clean.   You **can't** throw trash into the ocean.
> We **must** protect the oceans.   **Don't** leave food on the beach.

1 Read. Check the true sentences.

1. We must throw plastic bags in the ocean. ○
2. Don't leave trash in the classroom. ○
3. You have to throw trash in the rivers. ○
4. You can't use biodegradable things. They will never disappear. ○
5. We must protect natural habitats. ○

2 Read. Complete the sentences.

Protect Our Oceans!

1. We _____must_____ protect the whales and the dolphins.
2. We _____ throw bottles into the ocean.
3. _____ leave garbage on the beach.
4. We _____ respect and protect nature.
5. _____ use lots of plastic bags.
6. We _____ learn about our oceans and tell other people about them.

10 Unit 6

3 **Write.** What about you? Write about rules at home and at school.

At home, _____I must_____

_____

_____

_____

_____

At school, _____

_____

_____

_____

_____

4 **Compare your rules.** Discuss in pairs.

At school, don't leave garbage in the classroom.

At home, we must clean up.

VOCABULARY 2

1 Listen and repeat. Then read and write. TR: 6.5

oil spill   garbage   overfishing

plastic bags — not **biodegradable**

a paper bag — **biodegradable**

1. Banana peels, plastic bottles, soda cans, old newspapers, boxes, and broken toys are examples of _____.

2. When companies catch too many fish all the time, there aren't enough fish left to reproduce. This is called _____.

3. Paper is _____. With time, it disappears.

4. Bottles and bags made out of _____ are not biodegradable.

5. Big ships called *tankers* transport oil across the ocean. When they have an accident and oil escapes, the result is an _____.

2 Listen, talk, and stick. Work with a partner. TR: 6.6

Oil spills happen when tankers have accidents on the ocean.

Right.

1   2   3   4   5

12 Unit 6

GRAMMAR 2

Future with *will* and *won't* TR: 6.7

What **will** happen in the future?   Sea animals and plants **will** disappear.
We **won't** have as much food as we need.

1 Read and answer.

1. Oil pollution affects the sunlit zone of the ocean.
   What will happen if there is a big oil spill?

   _____

2. Pollution affects oxygen levels in the midnight zone and creates areas with no oxygen. Animals live in this area. What will happen to the animals?

   _____

3. Imagine there are no more fish in the ocean. What will happen if there are no more fish?

   _____

4. In some places, fishing boats catch too many fish.
   What will happen if overfishing happens for a long time?

   _____

2 Play a game. Cut out seven pictures and the bingo card in the back of the book. Listen and play. Discuss. TR: 6.8

This is not biodegradable.

Plastic!

READING

1 Listen and read. TR: 6.9

Colorful Corals

A coral reef looks like a colorful underwater garden. But corals are not plants. Corals are made up of tiny animals called *polyps*. Polyps have soft, transparent bodies without bones.

What's for dinner? Polyps have a mouth, stomach, and tentacles to catch food. Some polyps live in warm, sunlit zones. In daylight, these polyps get food from tiny plants called *algae*. After dark, the polyps use their tentacles to catch food. Some corals can even catch fish! In contrast, polyps that live in cold, dark zones have to work harder. There are no algae, so they have to use their tentacles to catch tiny animals called *plankton* in the water.

Underwater communities. Most corals live together in huge groups called *colonies*. Some build a protective skeleton around themselves. Old generations die and new ones grow on top, slowly building up coral reefs. Some are millions of years old. These beautiful reefs are home to more than 4,000 kinds of fish and thousands of other organisms.

Save the reefs! Coral reefs provide food for communities. They are also a source of tourism and jobs for local people. Scientists use reef animals to develop new medicines. But coral reefs are in danger from pollution. Coral reefs are disappearing. Some experts predict that only 10 percent of the world's corals will exist in the year 2050. We must protect our corals now.

Okinawa, Japan

Weird but true

The Great Barrier Reef is more than 2,000 km (1,200 mi.) long! You can see it from outer space!

2 **Read.** Complete the definitions.

1. Corals are made up of individual animals called _____.

2. Warm-water polyps get food from tiny plants called _____.

3. Cold-water polyps eat tiny animals called _____.

4. Most corals live in very large groups called _____.

3 **Label.** Look and read the text again. Then write a label for each number.

1. _____

2. _____

3. _____

4 **Talk, listen, and write.** Choose warm or cold corals to talk to a partner about. Your partner will listen and complete the first column. Then listen to your partner and fill in the second column.

Type of coral		
They are made up of		
They live in		
They eat		

15

WRITING

> **Contrast Writing** In contrast writing, you write about the differences between two things. You can use facts and descriptive words to show differences. You can also use words that show contrast, such as *but* and *however*, and expressions such as *in contrast*.

1 **Read.** Read about land turtles and sea turtles. How does the writer show differences? Underline the words and expressions.

Land and Sea Turtles

All turtles begin their lives on land. Mother turtles lay their eggs in holes and then cover them up to protect them. But after that, the baby turtles' lives are very different. The baby land turtles crawl away to live in woods, swamps, grasslands, or deserts. In contrast, the baby sea turtles crawl to the ocean to live their lives in the water.

Land turtles and sea turtles look different, too. Land turtles have hard, high, round shells. When they are afraid, they hide in their shells. Sea turtles, however, have soft, flatter shells. They can't hide inside, but they can swim away really fast. When cold weather comes, land turtles dig holes in the ground and sleep. They are too slow to move to warmer places. In contrast, sea turtles simply swim away to find warmer waters.

land turtle

sea turtle

2 **Write.** Write about warm and cold corals. How are they different? Use words and expressions that show contrast.

3 **Share.** Share your writing in a small group. Listen and take notes.

Name	Warm corals	Cold corals
Jan	They get food from algae.	They catch all their food.

16 Unit 6

MISSION
Protect the oceans.

Think. Pair. Share.

- What will our oceans be like in 20 years?
- Why must we protect our oceans?
- What can we do to help?

Sipadan Island, Malaysia

"With every drop of water you drink, every breath you take, you're connected to the ocean – no matter where on Earth you live. Taking care of the ocean means taking care of us."

Dr. Sylvia Earle, Oceanographer, **National Geographic Explorer**

17

PROJECT

Make posters to help sea animals.

1. Research ways you can help sea animals.
2. Make posters.
3. Make cards to hand out.
4. Invite people to a community clean-up.
5. At your event, take photos for a school newspaper article.

> Our poster is about why it's important to protect coral reefs.

Now I can . . .

○ name and describe sea life.

○ talk about how we can protect the oceans.

○ talk about future events.

○ write to describe how things are different.

Save Our Oceans!

- Plastic is bad for our oceans. It's not biodegradable. It never disappears!
- Sea animals and birds eat plastic or get "caught" in it.
- We use plastic drinking straws for a short time, then we throw them away. If they get into the ocean, they stay there forever.
- Use paper straws. There are also straws made of bamboo or metal that you can use again and again. Or just **don't use a straw!**

Say **NO** to plastic straws and sea animals will thank you!

19

Unit 7
Good Idea!

Space projection helmets,
Washington, DC, USA

In this unit, I will . . .
- talk about inventions.
- talk about past habits.
- describe how to use an invention.
- write facts and opinions about a favorite invention.

Look and answer.

1. Where are these people?
2. What are they doing?
3. What are they wearing?
4. Write a caption for this photo.

VOCABULARY 1

1 **Listen and read.** TR: 7.1

2 **Listen and repeat.** TR: 7.2

Inventions are everywhere. Look around you. What inventions can you see?

One of the first inventions was the **wheel.** More than five thousand years ago, it was difficult to move things. People had to push or pull them along the ground. That was a **problem.** Then someone found a **solution**—the wheel. It changed our lives.

Electricity is not an invention. It always existed in nature—in lightning, for example. But scientists discovered it and worked out how to use it. Inventors used **imagination** and **creativity** to make new inventions such as electric lights. When **batteries** were **invented,** electricity became even more **useful.** Now we can't imagine our lives without battery-powered inventions such as computers and cell phones.

a battery

electricity

a wheel

22 Unit 7

Some inventions were invented too soon—years before they became really useful. One example was the windshield wiper. On a snowy day in 1903, Mary Anderson was riding in a streetcar in New York. From time to time, the driver had to open his window to wipe the snow from his windshield by hand. Back at home, Mary Anderson drew her **idea** for a windshield wiper. She **tried** to sell her invention, but **failed**. People thought windshield wipers could distract drivers and cause accidents!

Air travel is used by millions of people today. However, there's some discussion about who flew first. The Wright brothers tried to fly many times. They finally **succeeded** in 1903. But others say Alberto Santos-Dumont flew first. Santos-Dumont had the world's first public flight in 1906 outside of Paris. He flew his plane 220 meters (722 ft.).

3 **Ask and answer.** Work with a partner. What did you learn?

When did the Wright brothers fly a plane?

They flew a plane in 1903.

SONG

1 Listen, read, and sing. TR: 7.3

Inventions

**Creativity!
Electricity!
Creativity changes the world!**

Inventions solve problems.
Problems that we used to have are gone!
The wheel and the cell phone
help to make our world go around!

Inventions are useful,
every day, in every way.
Computers, cars, and airplanes
help to make our world go around.

CHORUS

You used to have to walk
to get from place to place.
Years ago, you could only talk
face to face.
You could take only boats
to get across the sea.
Now, we fly across the sky.
Inventions are the reason why.

CHORUS

Imagination and ideas
can change the world, every day.
Can you solve a problem?
Can you help our world today?

CHORUS

Lion lights.
Nairobi, Kenya

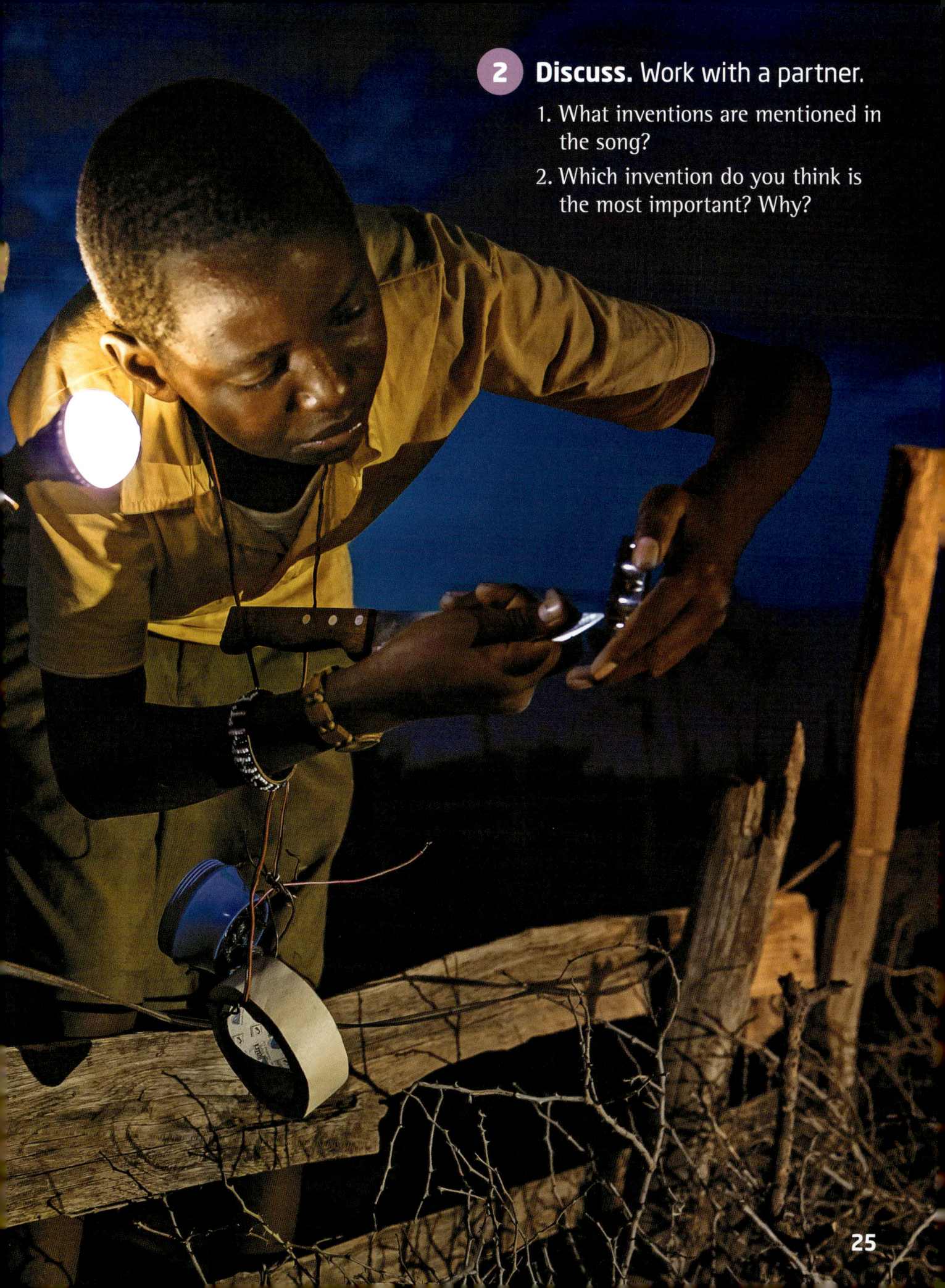

2 **Discuss.** Work with a partner.
1. What inventions are mentioned in the song?
2. Which invention do you think is the most important? Why?

GRAMMAR 1

Used to for past habits TR: 7.4

People **used to** travel across the sea in boats.

Why **did** people **use to** read by candlelight?

We **didn't use to** have airplanes.

They **didn't use to** have electricity.

1 **Read.** Complete the sentences. Check the true sentences.

1. In the 1980s, people _____ (read) by candlelight. _____

2. Before the invention of cars, people _____ _____ (ride) horses in the city. _____

3. Before the invention of the plane, people _____ _____ (not / travel) by air. _____

4. In the 1950s, people _____ (not / make) calls with a cell phone. _____

5. We _____ (not / have) computers before there was electricity. _____

2 **Ask and answer.** Work with a partner.

1. What did people use to do for fun before TV?
2. How did people use to travel before planes?
3. What did children use to play with before video games?

26 Unit 7

3 Write. What about you? Write five sentences about when you were younger. Write two that *aren't* true. Use these words to help you.

clothes   food   games   home
music   TV shows   toys   vacations
brothers and sisters   free-time activities

1. _____

_____

2. _____

_____

3. _____

_____

4. _____

_____

5. _____

_____

4 Read your sentences. Work with a partner. Take turns.

When I was six, I used to ride my bike to school.

That's not true! Your dad used to drive you to school. I saw you!

VOCABULARY 2

1 Listen and repeat. TR: 7.5
Complete. Then listen and check your answers. TR: 7.6

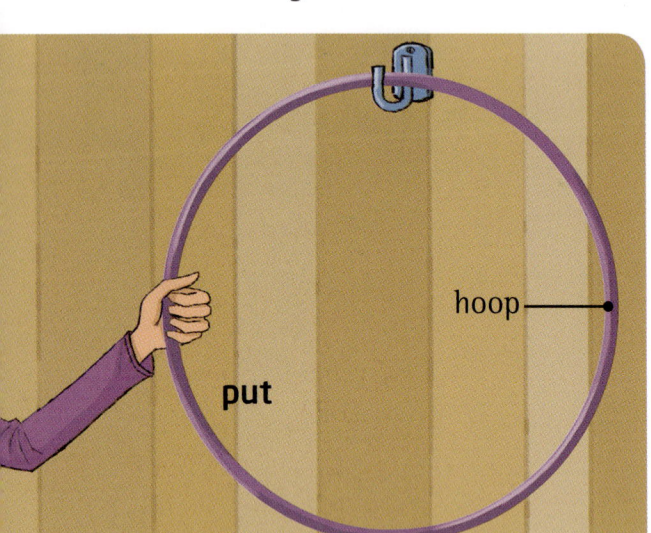

move

lift — waist

hoop
put

turn

use

The "hula hoop" is an old invention, but it's very popular today. It's fun and it's good exercise!

1. How do you _____ a hula hoop? It's easy. Follow these instructions.

2. _____ the hula hoop on the ground. Stand in the middle.

3. _____ the hoop to your waist.

4. _____ your waist in a circle. Don't hold the hoop!

5. The hoop _____ around and around. Can you feel it?

2 Listen and stick. Put the stickers in order. Then tell your partner how to use this toy. TR: 7.7

| 1 | 2 | 3 | 4 | 5 |

28 Unit 7

GRAMMAR 2

You for general statements TR: 7.8

You need to have creativity to invent things.
What do **you** do with this invention?

You should always try again if **you** fail.
Do **you** play with it?

1 Write clues about these inventions.

1. knife (cut meat) _You cut meat with it. You hold it in your hand._

2. microwave (cook food) _____

3. backpack (carry things) _____

4. cell phone (make calls) _____

5. scissors (cut paper) _____

6. crayons (color pictures) _____

2 **Play a game.** Work with a partner. Cut out the game board in the back of the book. Ask questions about the inventions you see. Take turns.

Heads = 1 space

Tails = 2 spaces

What's this?

It's an umbrella.

How do you use it?

You put it over your head when it's raining.

29

READING

1 Listen and read. TR: 7.9

YOUNG and Creative

Did you know that a teenager had the first idea for a television? And a six-year-old boy invented the toy truck? Kids and teens are great inventors because they have a lot of creativity and imagination.

2018: At the age of 19, Angad Daryani invented a solution to the problem of air pollution in cities. Growing up in Mumbai, India, he suffered from asthma caused by the polluted air. Air pollution is a big problem. Three million people die each year. Angad's invention is an air pollution cleaning tower that is 6.1 meters (20 ft.) high. The tower sucks in air and takes out the particles of dust and carbon. The particles are collected and can even be reused. Angad's dream is to build thousands of the towers and improve the quality of air in cities.

2013: Canadian high school student Ann Makosinski was 15 when she invented the "hollow flashlight." The flashlight uses heat from the human body and changes it into light. It doesn't need batteries. Ann thought of the idea when she heard about a friend who lived in the Philippines. Her friend was doing badly in school. She needed to do her homework at night, but there was no electrical light in her home. Ann's flashlight isn't expensive. Ann hopes it will help some of the 1.1 billion people in the world who still have no electricity in their homes.

1905: When Frank Epperson was eleven, he left a cup filled with soda and a stick in his yard. That night he forgot about it. It was a very cold night. When he went outside the next morning, he found something amazing: a "Popsicle"!

1824: Louis Braille had an accident when he was three. The accident left him blind. At that time, it was hard for blind children to read. They had to touch raised letters. But it was easy to confuse a Q with an O, an R with a B, and so on. When he was fifteen, Louis invented an alphabet that used raised dots. The Braille alphabet was a big success!

2 Read and write. Write the name of the invention.

1. It's something you eat. _____

2. It can help people who live in big cities. _____

3. It's something a blind person can use to read. _____

4. It's useful if you don't have electricity. _____

5. It happened by accident. _____

3 Read and write. Complete the chart.

Who	When	What	Why
Angad Daryani	in 2018, when he was 19 years old	an air pollution cleaning tower	He had asthma caused by air pollution.

4 Discuss the questions. Work in groups of three. Do you have the same opinion?

Which story was the most interesting? Why?

Which invention was the most useful? Why?

NUMBER OF PATENT FILINGS AROUND THE WORLD

Diane Bisson invented a series of healthy and tasty plates and bowls that you can eat!

31

WRITING

> **Fact and Opinion Writing** In fact and opinion writing, you state your opinion and use facts to support your opinion. An *opinion* is something you believe to be true. To introduce opinions, use words like *in my opinion, I think,* and *I believe.* A *fact* is a piece of true information, for example, a date, an event, or a name.

1 **Read.** Read this fact and opinion text. Underline facts that support the opinion in the first paragraph.

A Good Idea

In my opinion, sticky notes are a great invention. They're easy to use. You write a note and stick it on your notebook or on your computer. And they come off easily. I think most people like them because they help you to remember things.

In my opinion, the story of sticky notes is interesting, too. Sticky notes have two inventors. Spencer Silver invented the glue in 1970. It wasn't strong, so he didn't know how to use it. But four years later, Arthur Fry found a use for it. One day, all his notes fell on the floor. He wasn't happy! Then he remembered Silver's glue! He used the glue on small pieces of paper. It worked! You could stick the notes to almost any surface, and it was easy to remove them. Now we have a cool—and useful—invention!

Use my imagination!

COOL invention!

2 **Write.** Describe an invention. Explain how to use it and why you like it. Include facts to support your opinion.

3 **Share.** Share your writing. Work in a group. Listen and take notes.

Invention	How do we use it?	Why does he/she like it?
Peanut butter	We eat it.	It's delicious.

MISSION

Use your imagination and creativity to solve problems.

The Sheep View project equipped sheep with solar-powered 360-degree cameras. The Faroe Islands are now part of street-view maps online.

Think. Pair. Share.

- What are some typical problems in your daily life?

- Can you solve any of them with an invention? Note any useful or fun ideas.

- Which inventions does everyone like best? Discuss as a class.

"In science, it's always a long train of ideas. Many succeed, but in between you often fail . . . science is entirely based on curiosity."

Aydogan Ozcan, Electrical Engineer, **National Geographic Explorer**

PROJECT

Design a superpower app.

1. Choose your own superpower—something that makes life better. Design an app to help you achieve it.

2. Sketch out your ideas for your app in 3-4 pictures.

3. Share your ideas in a small group. Ask your friends how you can improve your ideas.

4. Present your finished app design to the class.

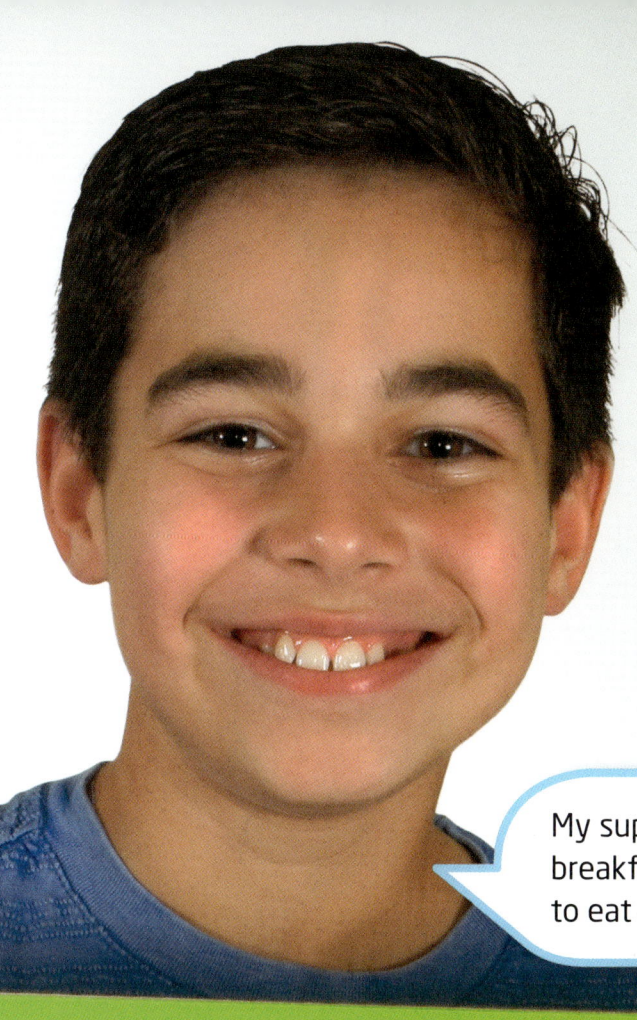

Now I can . . .

○ talk about inventions.

○ talk about past habits.

○ describe how to use an invention.

○ write facts and opinions about a favorite invention.

My superhero is Superfood Man. I didn't use to eat breakfast, but now I do! Superfood Man reminds me to eat a healthy breakfast every morning. He's great!

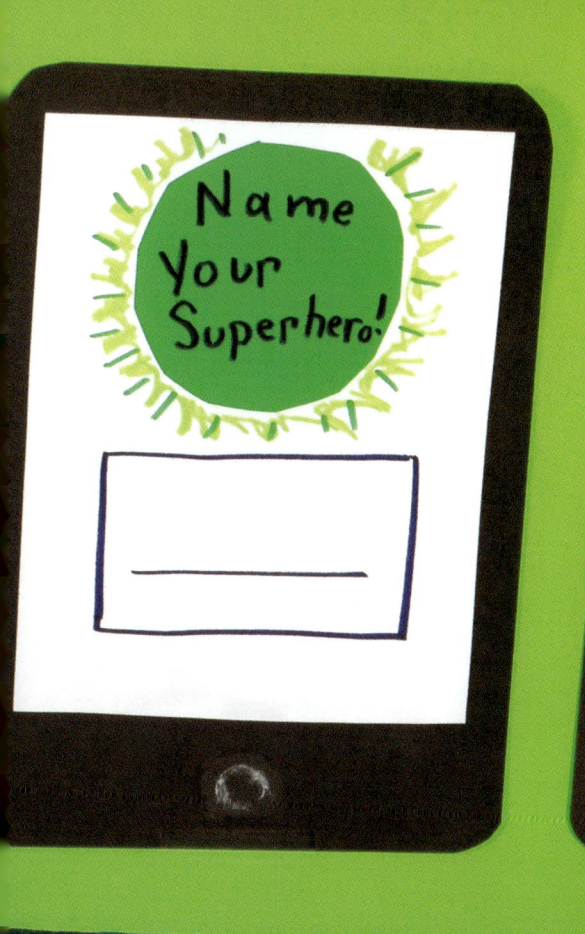

Unit 8

That's Really Interesting!

In this unit, I will . . .
- talk about my hobbies and interests.
- give information about people I know.
- talk about gifts I've received.
- describe and explain a hobby.

Look and check.

Who is taking the photo?

◯ a photographer

◯ a hiker

◯ a polar bear

Write a caption for this photo.

_____

A curious polar bear investigating a photographer's camera. Svalbard, Norway

VOCABULARY 1

1 **Listen and read.** TR: 8.1

2 **Listen and say.** TR: 8.2

Most people have a hobby. Some children **collect** things, play in a **musical group,** or grow vegetables. **Creative** people often paint or **take photos.** Video games are popular, too. What hobbies do you **enjoy?**

Many video games are for one person. You play **alone.** But it's more fun to play with a friend. Choose your **avatars.** Then **compete.** To win the game, you must get many **points.** The person with the highest **score** wins.

In other video games, you play **together** with a friend. You don't compete. You **cooperate.** When you use the **controller,** you can see your avatars move on the **screen.**

Bisate Village, Rwanda

a screen

points

a score

an avatar

a controller

3 **Ask and answer.** Work with a partner. What did you learn?

What do creative people do?

They often paint or take photos.

39

SONG

1 **Listen, read, and sing.** TR: 8.3

What's Your Hobby?

What's your hobby?
What do you like to do?
What's your hobby?
I have a hobby, too!

The boy who has the highest score
wins the video game.
The girl who collects a fossil
wants to learn its name.
Who enjoys a comic book?
Who likes to compete?
I collect stuffed animals
because I think they're sweet.

CHORUS

The boy who takes a photo
sees it on the screen.
The girl who reads about dinosaurs
can see them in her dreams.
Do you like to cooperate?
Do you like to work alone?
I like to talk about my hobby
on my new cell phone.

It's fun to be creative and show what you can do.
Collect, compete, cooperate.
I have a hobby.
Do you?

CHORUS

2 **Answer.** Work with a partner.

1. Which hobbies are mentioned in the song?
2. Which of these hobbies do you like?

Istanbul, Turkey

MÜDÜRLÜGÜ
MÜDÜRLÜGÜ
İSTANBUL İLİ
SİNANPAŞA MEDRESESİ ve CAMİİ
ÇEVRE DÜZENLEMESİ
(RESTORASYON) İŞİ

GRAMMAR 1

Describing people with *who* TR: 8.4

The person **who** has the highest score wins the game.
I know a boy **who** collects movie posters.
We have three cousins **who** play in a musical group together.

1 **Read and write.** Join the two sentences.

1. I have a younger brother. He loves video games.

   I have a younger brother who loves video games.

2. There is a girl in my class. She collects seashells.

   _____

3. My best friend is a creative person. She takes amazing photos.

   _____

4. I have an aunt. She's very creative.

   _____

5. I know three people. They collect fossils.

   _____

Trilobite fossil, Morocco

42 Unit 8

2 **Do a class survey.** Ask questions. Write names and count. Then write about the people in your class on a sheet of paper.

Who . . .	Name(s)
1. enjoys books?	
2. likes to compete in sports?	
3. likes to play video games?	
4. often takes photos?	
5. has more than one hobby?	
6. collects something?	

There are three students who enjoy books. They are Maria, Carlos, and Tomas.

3 **Ask and answer.** Work in a group. Talk about someone in your class. Don't say the name. Can your group guess who it is?

This person is someone who enjoys books and often takes photos. Who is it?

Is it Tomas?

No, it isn't. Try again!

VOCABULARY 2

1 Listen and repeat. Check T for *True* and F for *False*. TR: 8.5

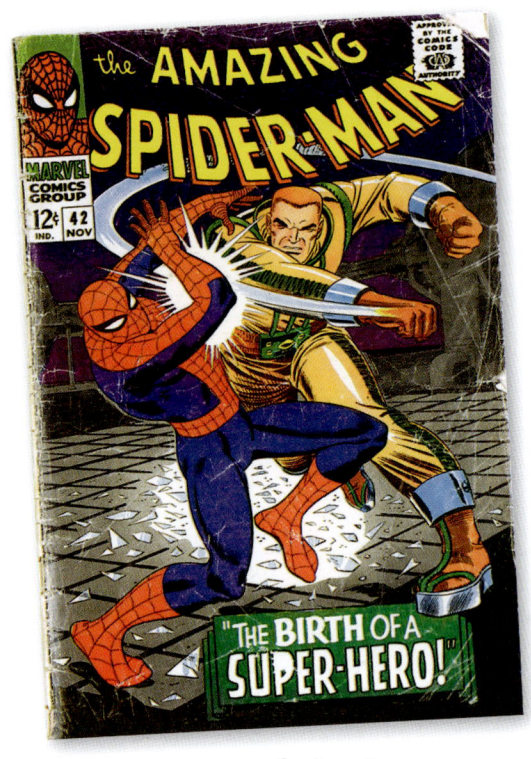

a comic book

a bug

a dinosaur

a fossil

a stuffed animal

1. She's scared of bugs.   T   F
2. She thinks dinosaurs are boring.   T   F
3. She knows a boy who collects comic books.   T   F
4. Her brother collects fossils.   T   F
5. Her dad gave her a stuffed animal for her birthday.   T   F

2 Ask and answer. Work with a partner. It's party time. What present did you give? Stick.

What did you give Maria?

I gave her a pair of socks.

How boring! I gave her a doll!

1   2   3   4   5

GRAMMAR 2

> **Direct and indirect objects** TR: 8.6
> Show <u>the comic book</u> **to James.** = Show **James** <u>the comic book</u>.
> My dad gave <u>this fossil</u> **to me.** = My dad gave **me** <u>this fossil</u>.
> My mom bought <u>stuffed animals</u> **for them.** = My mom bought **them** <u>stuffed animals</u>.

1 Read and write. Rewrite the sentences.

1. My cousin sent a dinosaur book to him.

   My cousin sent him a dinosaur book.

2. When I was in the hospital, my uncle gave a stuffed animal to me.

   _____

3. He became friends with two kids and gave two comic books to them.

   _____

4. Grandma sent a present to him, and he wrote a letter to her.

   _____

2 Play a game. Cut out the game board and the cube in the back of the book. Work with a partner. Take turns.

My friend gave me a toy dinosaur!

Yes, he gave a toy dinosaur to me.

Really?

me = 1 space 😊
him/her/them = 0 spaces 😞

45

READING

1 Listen and read. TR: 8.7

HIDE and SEEK

Geocaching is a fun outdoor hobby. It's like a game of hide and seek, with the hiders leaving clues for the seekers to find. Here's how it works: The hiders hide a box, or *cache*. Inside the box, they put some "treasure"—small objects for you to find—and a notebook. If you want to be a seeker, or geocacher, you use an app that tells you where there are caches near you.

Then you look for the cache. To help you find it, you need to have your smartphone with online clues, or a map and compass. You should also take a pen or pencil and a few small treasures to leave for other people.

When you find the cache, you look for the notebook inside. Then you write your name and the date. Then you look at the treasures in the box and choose something you like to take away. You might choose a small toy, an ornament, or a little book. Don't forget to leave another treasure in its place!

Geocaching is a great way to explore new places and make new friends. Many geocachers also help to clean up the places they visit by picking up garbage they see along the way.

One geocacher says it's a great hobby because "It gets the whole family outside and doing something fun together. I love it!"

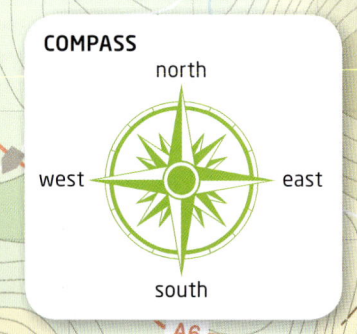

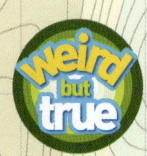

COMPASS
north
west east
south

Weird but true
A Japanese sailor sent a message in a bottle when his boat was sinking. The message asked for help. About 150 years later, the bottle arrived in the town where he was born!

46 Unit 8

2 **Read.** Put the geocaching steps in order.

_____ You write your name and the date.

_____ You look for the notebook.

_____ You leave an object in the box for someone else to find.

_____ You choose a treasure to take away.

_____ You find the cache and open it.

3 **Write.** Label the pictures.

a. map   **b.** ~~toys~~   **c.** notebook   **d.** water bottle
e. app   **f.** compass   **g.** clue   **h.** pen/pencil

b

4 **Discuss.** Work in a group. What should people take with them when they go geocaching? Write your ideas in the chart.

Very Important	Important	Not Important

47

WRITING

Explanation Writing When you write an explanation, you describe something in general. You explain what it is and how you do it. You can explain difficult words and give examples. Use words and expressions like *for example* and *such as*.

1 Read. Read this explanation. Underline definitions and examples.

Fun with Paper

The Japanese invented origami in the 17th century, and now it is popular everywhere in the world.

The word "origami" comes from two Japanese words: "ori," which means "folding," and "kami," which means "paper." In origami, you always begin with one square sheet of paper. Then you fold the paper many times to make a shape.

Origami is very creative. You can make simple shapes, for example, a little bug. Or you can make a difficult design. To make a difficult shape, such as a dragon, you have to fold the paper many times in different ways. The most famous origami design is the Japanese paper crane. Origami isn't always easy, but it's fun!

crane

frog

dinosaur

2 Write. Describe a hobby. Explain it and how to do it.

3 Share. Share your writing in a small group. Listen and take notes.

Name	Hobby	What and how
Filip	Photography	Take interesting photos. Use a camera or phone.

48 Unit 8

MISSION

Enjoy a hobby.

Think. Pair. Share.

- Why is it good to have a hobby?

- What hobby would you like to try, and why?

- How do you do the hobby you chose? What do you need?

Ammonite fossils

"As a child, I felt very alone with my interest in fossils. Finally, at age 13, I discovered there was a museum in Norway that actually employed people to study fossils."

Jørn Hurum, Paleontologist, **National Geographic Explorer**

PROJECT

Present a hobby.

1 Choose one of your favorite hobbies or interests.

2 Prepare a report for the class.

   a. Explain details about it.

   b. Explain how you do it.

   c. Use drawings or photos. You can also bring objects to show the class.

> This is the coolest rock I have! I bought it on vacation.

GEODES

- Geodes are beautiful round rocks.
- We can find them near rivers.
- They take 240 million years to form.

Smooth light gray rock.

Lined with sparkling minerals.

Geodes in their natural form.

's largest Geode in Crystal Caves.

A close up of the crystals.

Quartz crystals

Mexico

USA

Brazil

Geodes

Now I can . . .

○ talk about my hobbies and interests.

○ give information about people I know.

○ talk about gifts I've received.

○ describe and explain a hobby.

51

Unit 9

The Science of Fun

Roberts Creek, British Columbia, Canada

In this unit, I will . . .
- identify how we use force to move.
- use *The more* . . . to describe cause and effect.
- understand and make definitions.
- write about cause and effect.

Look and answer.

1. What is he doing?

2. Is it easy?

3. What special clothes is he wearing, and why?

4. Write a caption for the photo.

_____

_____

53

VOCABULARY 1

1 **Listen and read.** TR: 9.1

2 **Listen and repeat.** TR: 9.2

We use **force** to move. Force **happens** when we **push** or **pull**. Do you push or pull when you move on a **swing?** You do both.

Look at this **skier**. To move, a skier pushes on the snow. A push can move a skier **forward**. It can also move a skier **backward**.

forward

skaters

Skaters pull, too. Look at these skaters. The more one skater pulls, the more they **spin**. The skaters don't **fall over** because they know how to **balance**.

How do skaters stop? They use force. Skaters push **down** hard on their skates. The skates **connect** with the ice. The ice and skates **rub** together. When two things rub together, it's called **friction**.

backward

How do skaters stop?

They use force.

3 **Ask and answer.**
Work with a partner.
What did you learn?

55

SONG

1 **Listen, read, and sing.** TR: 9.3

I'm on the Move!

Push it, pull it, push it, pull it, push, pull.
Push, pull, push, pull! Watch it go!

If you spin around, and around and around
and around,
what you feel is force.
If you fall down, down, down, down,
down to the ground,
that's gravity, of course.

**I'm on the move.
I'm in the groove.
It's amazing what you can do
when you let force do the work for you!**

The more you push, the faster some things go.
When you spin around, the force comes and goes.

CHORUS

The more you push, the faster some things go.
When you spin around, the force comes and goes.

Push it, pull it, push it, pull it, push, pull.
Push, pull, push, pull! Watch it go!

If you spin around, and around and around
and around,
what you feel is force.
If you fall down, down, down, down,
down to the ground,
that's gravity, of course.

CHORUS

I'm on the move!

Our Dynamic Earth bootcamp, Edinburgh, Scotland

2 Answer. Work with a partner.

1. How do you feel when you spin? And when you fall?
2. Look at the photo. What is the boy doing?

GRAMMAR 1

Cause and effect with double comparatives TR: 9.4

The more one skater pulls, **the more** the other one spins.
The more you push the swing, **the faster** it goes.
The more you practice, **the faster** you run.

1 **Match the pictures to the first part of the sentences.**
Then match to complete the sentences.

The more they spin,   the higher he goes.

The more she pushes,   the higher she goes.

The more he pushes down,   the faster they go.

2 **Read and write.** Complete the sentences.

1. The more he goes down, _the more she goes up._

2. The more she goes up, _____.

3. The more he goes around, _____.

4. The more she spins, _____.

58 Unit 9

3 **Read and write.** Complete the sentences.

1. _The more she pushes_, (she / push) on the swing, _the higher she goes_. (high / she / go)

2. _____, (the skateboarder / push) _____. (fast / he / move forward)

3. _____, (high / she / go) _____. (she / feel dizzy)

4. _____, (you / play soccer) _____. (good / you / get)

5. _____, (we / practice) _____. (we / win)

4 **Talk to a partner.** Imagine you are having fun. Describe what happens to you.

ball	climb	fast	force	good
high	jump	laugh	play	practice
pull	push	soccer	win	

The more you practice, the faster you run!

The more you play, the more you laugh!

59

VOCABULARY 2

1 Listen and repeat. Read and write. Complete the sentences. TR: 9.5

1. When you throw a ball, _____ pulls it toward the Earth.

2. Don't go in that _____ . Turn left!

3. He is walking _____ the music because it's too loud.

4. When you ride your bicycle and want to turn left, you turn your wheel to the left, and you _____ to the left.

5. She is riding _____ the swings because she wants to play on them.

2 Listen and stick. Work with a partner. Compare your answers. TR: 9.6

| 1 | 2 | 3 | 4 | 5 |

60 Unit 9

GRAMMAR 2

Definitions with *which* TR: 9.7
Gravity is a force **which** pulls you toward Earth.
Skates are special shoes **which** you wear when you go ice skating.

1 **Write a definition for each item.** Work with a partner. Read your definitions and guess. Take turns.

1. Bicycle: This is a machine <u>which you can ride in the park.</u>

2. Skateboarding: It is a hobby _____.

3. Friction: This is a force _____.

4. Tetherball: It is a game _____.

5. Soccer: This is a sport _____.

2 **Play a game.** Play with a partner. Cut out the cards in the back of the book. Follow the instructions. Take turns.

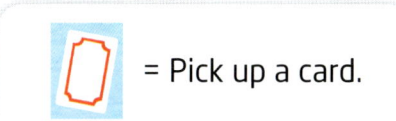

▯ = Pick up a card.

A bicycle is a machine with wheels and handlebars which you ride.

OK! My turn!

READING

1 Listen and read. TR: 9.8

Up, Down, and All Around!

You are going on a roller-coaster ride. Sit in the car and pull down the safety bar. Are you ready? Let's go!

First you go up a steep hill. The roller coaster goes slow. Next gravity pulls you down the hill. The roller coaster moves fast. You feel very light!

A big circle, known as the "loop the loop," is many people's favorite. When you go fast up the circle, you feel heavy. Gravity is pulling you down. When you reach the top, you are high in the sky. And you're hanging upside down! So why don't you fall out of your seat? Your body wants to fly off, but the speed of the car and a force called *centripetal force* keep you moving in a circle, and keep you in your seat!

The roller coaster uses friction to stop. If it stops quickly, your body wants to continue moving. That is called inertia. But the safety bars keep you in place!

Not everyone loves roller coasters. They make some people feel dizzy or sick because the forces change. In fact, we experience forces like friction, centripetal force, and gravity every day. For example, you feel gravity when you jump with your bike and come down. You feel centripetal force when you turn, and you feel friction when you use the brakes to stop the bike.

How do you want to experience the forces? Do you want to ride your bicycle or a roller coaster?

Weird but true
Russians invented the roller coaster. They made the "cars" from ice. And they put straw on the seats to keep the passengers warm.

2 **Answer the questions.** Work with a partner.

1. What is the first thing you do when you sit in a roller coaster?

2. How do you feel when you go fast down the hill?

3. How do you feel when you go fast up the loop the loop?

4. Why do some people feel dizzy or sick on roller coasters?

3 **Complete the chart.** Work with a partner. When do you experience these forces in roller coasters and on bicycles?

	Roller coaster	Bicycle
Gravity		
Centripetal force		
Friction		
Inertia		

4 **Look and discuss.** Work with a partner. Describe a ride on a roller coaster.

- What does the roller coaster look like?
- It looks like a spaceship!
- What happens first?
- You go straight toward the sky, but then you turn!

WRITING

> **Cause and Effect Writing** When you write about cause and effect, you describe actions and tell why they happened. Use *because* or *as* to show cause. You also describe the effect of the action. To show effect, you use words like *so*, *so that*, and *as a result*.

1 **Read.** How does the writer describe cause and effect? Underline the words and phrases.

Last week I learned how to play tetherball with my brother. My brother plays a lot, so he taught me. We went to the park because there's a new tetherball court there.

As there aren't many rules, it's easy to start playing tetherball. Two people play the game. One person hits the ball to the right. The other person hits it to the left. Because the rope is connected to a pole, the ball can't fly away. You hit the ball so that it turns around the pole. Tetherball looks easy. But it isn't.

Last week I hit the ball, it flew around in a big circle. As a result, it was easy for my brother to hit it. Then he hit the ball. It went fast and very high so that I couldn't hit it. So he won every game. Because I want to win next time, I'm going to practice a lot from now on!

2 **Write.** Describe a favorite game. Say why you play it and what happens when you play. Include words of cause and effect.

3 **Share.** Share your writing in a small group. Listen and take notes.

Name	Game	How to do or play it
Isabelle	jumping rope	Jump over the rope each time it turns.

MISSION

Think creatively and critically.

Think. Pair. Share.

- Why is it important to understand how and why things work?

- How can we learn more about how and why things work?

- Think of three examples of things you would like to understand better.

"When something unexpected or unusual happens, I am always curious to find out why."

Stephon Alexander, Theoretical Physicist, **National Geographic Explorer**

PROJECT

Make a thaumatrope.

1. Cut out two circles of cardstock paper or cardboard. Make them the same size.

2. Draw an object, person, or animal in the middle of one circle.

3. Draw a "home" for the object, person, or animal on the other circle.

4. Stick or glue the two circles together. The picture on the back should be upside down.

5. Make holes on each side. Attach string or a rubber band.

6. Spin the circles fast and watch the two pictures turn into one! Why do you think this happens?

Now I can . . .

○ identify how we use force to move.

○ use *The more . . .* to describe cause and effect.

○ understand and make definitions.

○ write about cause and effect.

I drew a fish on one circle, and a fish tank on the other. When I spin it, it looks like the fish is in the tank!

EXTENDED READING

1 Listen and read. TR: 6.12

Oceans of Plastic: TIME FOR ACTION

Plastic is useful. It's in a lot of things we use every day, from clothes to pens, and bottles to toys. But there's a problem. Most plastic is not biodegradable, and a lot of it ends up in our oceans.

How big is the problem?

There are likely more than 5 trillion—that's 5,000,000,000,000!—bits of plastic in the world's oceans. Every ocean and every beach has plastic, from large objects to tiny pieces called *microplastics*. Tons of plastic enter the ocean every year. At this rate, by 2050 there will be more plastic than fish in our oceans!

How does plastic harm animals?

Fish, sea turtles, and birds think plastic is food, and they eat it. The plastic stays in their stomachs. Dead seabirds are found with stomachs full of plastic. Whales, dolphins, and seals get tangled up in plastic packaging or fishing nets. It's estimated that millions of ocean animals die each year because of plastic garbage in oceans around the world.

Is there any good news?

Yes! Scientists, schools, businesses, and everyday people are taking action. Some countries have banned plastic bags. Scientists are developing new biodegradable plastics. Many communities are trying to use less plastic and recycle more. Kids and young people are playing their part, too, from Boyan Slat, 23, who is developing an ocean sweeping machine, to kids around the world working to make their schools "zero plastic."

What can you do?
- Don't use plastic bags.
- Don't litter.
- Don't use plastic straws.
- Get a refillable water bottle. Don't buy plastic bottles.
- Recycle.

One person can't solve the problem alone, but together we will make a difference.

2 Read. Match to make sentences.

1. Plastic in our oceans
2. In 2050, our oceans could have
3. Each year millions of ocean animals
4. Kids and young people

a. more plastic than fish.
b. are helping solve the problem.
c. is a very big problem.
d. die because of plastic.

3 Read. Answer the questions. Work with a partner.

1. How do you think plastic gets into the oceans?
2. Which do you think are harder to clean up—large plastic objects or tiny pieces? Which do more harm?
3. How are people taking action? Which actions do you think are the most important?

4 Read. Express yourself. Choose an activity.

1. Choose a marine animal or seabird. Draw or paint a picture of it, then label it, showing how plastic affects it.
2. Write and act out a play about plastic pollution.
3. Make a poster to persuade supermarkets to use less plastic.

EXTENDED READING

1 Listen and read. TR: 9.11

Leonardo da Vinci
The Greatest Inventor in History?

It is often told how Leonardo da Vinci used to go to his local market to buy birds in cages. Others bought the birds to kill and eat them, or keep them as pets. But Leonardo, to everyone's surprise, bought the birds to release from their cages and let them fly away!

Leonardo's kindness to animals was well known. He was a vegetarian. But more than this, he was fascinated by the flight of birds. Before releasing the birds, he studied their wing shape, structure, and movement. He made detailed drawings of birds' wings. Most of all, he had a dream—to design a machine that would let human beings fly like birds.

One of Leonardo's designs for a flying machine showed an enormous pair of wings joined to a wooden frame. According to the drawings, the brave pilot would lie inside the frame and move the wings up and down! Leonardo also drew a design for a glider. This was much simpler, and people have recently built and successfully flown it, with one small change to the original design. Other flight-related designs by Leonardo were for a helicopter and a parachute.

Leonardo was so many things—artist, musician, architect, engineer, scientist, and inventor. Today he is usually best known for his art, including two of the most famous paintings in the world: *Mona Lisa* and *The Last Supper*. However, centuries ahead of his time, he imagined and designed a huge range of inventions. Surely he must count as one of the greatest inventors ever?

LEONARDO DA VINCI'S LIFE

1452	1467	1482	1500
Leonardo da Vinci is born in Anchiano, Italy.	Young Leonardo goes to Florence to study with artist Andrea del Verrocchio.	Leonardo goes to Milan to work for the city's duke as a painter and engineer.	Leonardo returns to Florence and studies mathematics.

70 Extended Reading

2 Read the text again. Complete the sentences.

> 1519   flying   helicopter   paintings   released

1. Leonardo bought birds at the market and _____ them.

2. He studied the birds' wings so he could design a _____ machine.

3. Leonardo also designed a _____ and a parachute.

5. *Mona Lisa* is one of the most famous _____ in the world.

6. Leonardo lived from 1452 to _____.

3 Read. Answer the questions. Work with a partner.

1. Why were people surprised when Leonardo released the birds he had bought?

2. Which of Leonardo's inventions is the most important, in your opinion?

3. Leonardo's inventions were probably not made in his lifetime. Why not?

4 Express yourself. Choose an activity.

1. Look at pictures of some of Leonardo's inventions. Choose an invention of your own, and draw it in the same style as Leonardo's works. Add labels.

2. Imagine a scene at the market when Leonardo buys some caged birds. What do people say? What happens next? Write a short play. Work in a small group to act it out.

3. Make a poster of Leonardo's inventions alongside the same inventions in the modern day. Draw or paint, or find pictures and glue them on the poster. Label the inventions with the similarities and differences between now and then.

1502
Leonardo works for Cesare Borgia as an architect, map-maker, and engineer.

1503
Leonardo begins his most famous painting, *Mona Lisa*.

1503-1513
Leonardo studies flight, the human body, and rocks and plants.

1516-1519
Leonardo moves to France. He dies there.

Let's Talk

Hello!

I will . . .
- greet people (formally and informally).
- say thank you (formally and informally).

1 Listen and read. TR: 3.11

Sofia: **Hello,** Mrs. Gomez. **How are you?**
Mrs. Gomez: **I'm very well, thank you,** Sofia. Please come in.
Sofia: Thank you.

Sofia: **Hi,** Carla! **What's up?**
Carla: **Not much.** Hey, do you want a soda?
Sofia: Sure! **Thanks.**

Hello. Good morning. Good afternoon. Good evening.	**How are you?** How are you today?	**I'm very well, thank you.** I'm fine, **thanks.**
Hi! Hi there! Hey!	**What's up?** What are you doing? How're you doing? How's it going?	**Not much.** Nothing. Fine. I'm cool. / I'm good. Not bad.

2 Talk to a partner. Greet each other. Use the chart. Take turns.

I agree!

I will . . .
- ask for other people's opinions.
- agree and disagree.
- make generalizations.

3 **Listen and read.** TR: 3.12

Cho: **What do you think about** making a poster?
Jong: I think that's a great idea.
Mun-Hee: **I agree.** Posters are fun.
Jin: Really? **I disagree. Everybody makes posters!**
Hyo: **I think so, too.**

What do you think (about) _____?	I agree. I agree with (Jong). Great idea!	I think so, too.
	I disagree.	Everybody makes _____.
Let's do a (report). What do you think?	Not again! Let's do something else.	Surveys are cool.
	Really? I don't think so.	Reports are boring.

4 **Listen.** You will hear two discussions. Read each question and circle the answer. TR: 3.13

1. How many students want to do a survey?
   a. 1   b. 2   c. 3

2. How many students want to write a report?
   a. 1   b. 2   c. 3

5 **Prepare and practice discussions.** Work in groups of four.
- Preparing a talk about dinosaurs
- Making a poster about vegetables
- Doing a survey about chores

73

Let's Talk

What's wrong?

I will . . .
- ask how someone is feeling.
- describe how I feel.
- show that I care or understand.
- make a suggestion.

1 **Listen and read.** TR: 6.13

Aziz: **What's wrong?**
Sawsan: **I feel sick.**
Aziz: **Oh, no.** What's the problem?
Sawsan: I have a stomachache.
Aziz: **Why don't you** tell Mom?
Sawsan: Yeah, that's a good idea. Mom!

What's wrong?	I feel sick.	Oh, no.	Why don't you _____?
Hey, what's up?	I don't feel good.	I'm sorry.	You should _____.
What's the problem?	I'm not feeling well.	Oh, I'm really sorry.	Maybe you should _____.
What's the matter?	I'm tired.	That's too bad.	
	I'm hungry.		
	I'm mad at my brother.		

2 **Ask and answer with a partner.** Describe how you feel. Use the chart. Take turns.

I don't understand.

I will . . .
- politely interrupt.
- express confusion.
- check that someone understands.
- thank someone and reply.

3 **Listen and read.** TR: 6.14

Nikolai: Let's start the game.
Olga: **Hang on! I'm lost.** How do we play?
Nikolai: First you have to spin the spinner. Then you move your counter. **Got it?**
Olga: Yeah, **I think so. Thanks.**
Nikolai: **No problem.**

Hang on!	I'm lost.	Got it?	I think so.	No problem.
Wait a moment, please. Wait. Wait a minute / second. Hold on.	I don't understand. I don't get it.	Does that make sense? Does that help? OK?	Thanks. Oh, I see! Thanks. Oh, I get it now. Thanks.	You're welcome. That's OK. Sure!

4 **Listen.** You will hear two discussions. Read each question and circle the answer. TR: 6.15

1. Does the boy understand the instructions after the girl explains them?
   a. yes   b. no

2. Which expression does the boy use?
   a. Do you see now?   b. Got it?   c. OK?

5 **Practice discussions with a partner.** Imagine you are playing one of these games. One student doesn't understand. The other explains.

1. Tic-tac-toe
2. Bingo
3. Rock, paper, scissors

Let's Talk

Wow, that's cool!

I will . . .
- ask questions.
- show I'm interested.
- keep the conversation going.

1 **Listen and read.** TR: 9.12

Pablo: What's your favorite sport?
Mario: Soccer. I want to be a professional soccer player.
Pablo: **Do you?**
Mario: Yeah! **What about you?** What's your favorite sport?
Pablo: I love soccer, too. My dad is taking me to the World Cup!
Mario: Wow! **That's so cool!**

| **Do you?** (Can you? / Are you?) Really? Wow. | **What about you?** How about you? And you? | **That's so cool!** That's amazing! How cool! |

2 **Talk.** Talk about your favorite hobby or person. Work with a partner. Use the chart.

What does that mean?

I will . . .
- interrupt someone (formally and informally).
- ask the meaning and ask how to spell or say something.
- explain a meaning and give a spelling.
- say that I don't know.

3 **Listen and read.** TR: 9.13

Antoni: **Hey,** Martina, **what does this** word **mean?**
Martina: **I don't know. I think it's a kind of** invention.
Antoni: Um, I don't think so.
Martina: Why don't you ask the teacher?
Antoni: **That's a good idea. Excuse me,** Ms. Biga. What does this word mean?

Hey, Excuse me, Mr. / Ms. / Mrs. _____.	What does _____ mean?	I think it's a kind of _____. I think it means _____. It's the opposite of _____.	I don't know. I'm not sure.	That's a good idea. Good point.
	How do you spell _____? How do you pronounce this word? How do you say _____?			

4 **Listen.** You will hear two discussions. Read each question and circle the answer. TR: 9.14

1. What does the boy want to know?
   a. the meaning   b. the spelling   c. the pronunciation

2. What does the girl want to know?
   a. the meaning   b. the spelling   c. the pronunciation

5 **Prepare and practice.** Work in pairs. You want to know the spelling, the meaning, or the pronunciation of a word. Ask your partner and then ask the teacher.

77

Unit 6
Wonders of the Sea

VOCABULARY 1

1 **Read and write.** Do the puzzle. Find the secret message.

creature
disappear
dolphin
layer
midnight
ocean
octopus
pollution
resource
sea sponge
sea turtle
shark
squid
sunlight
whale
zone

RAECERTU — C R E A T U R E (1)
RYLAE — ⬜⬜⬜⬜ (15)
SLNUITGH — ⬜⬜⬜⬜⬜⬜⬜⬜ (2)
HIDGINMT — ⬜⬜⬜⬜⬜⬜⬜⬜ (14, 7)
ZEON — ⬜⬜⬜⬜ (11)
HALWE — ⬜⬜⬜⬜⬜ (10, 9)
ASE TUTREL — ⬜⬜⬜⬜⬜⬜⬜⬜⬜ (8)
COPSTUO — ⬜⬜⬜⬜⬜⬜⬜ (12)
RSKAH — ⬜⬜⬜⬜⬜
LIONDHP — ⬜⬜⬜⬜⬜⬜⬜ (13)
UQISD — ⬜⬜⬜⬜⬜
ASE GEPONS — ⬜⬜⬜⬜⬜⬜⬜⬜⬜ (5)
LILTOUNOP — ⬜⬜⬜⬜⬜⬜⬜⬜⬜
CEEROSRU — ⬜⬜⬜⬜⬜⬜⬜⬜
PIEDARSAP — ⬜⬜⬜⬜⬜⬜⬜⬜⬜ (4, 3)
ACNOE — ⬜⬜⬜⬜⬜ (6)

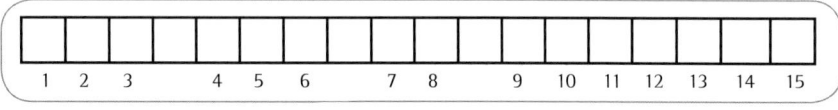

⬜⬜⬜ ⬜⬜⬜ ⬜⬜⬜⬜ ⬜⬜⬜⬜⬜⬜
1 2 3   4 5 6   7 8 9 10   11 12 13 14 15

2 **Listen.** Check the sea creatures that the girl saw at the aquarium. TR: 6.1

- ✓ squid
- dolphin
- octopus
- sea turtle
- shark

78 Unit 6

3. Read. Then match the questions and answers.

1. What's your favorite sea creature?
2. What time is it?
3. What do you need to grow vegetables?
4. Why is it an hour later in Sydney than in Tokyo?
5. OK. You have chocolate ice cream. What do you want next?

a. I'd like a layer of bananas with vanilla ice cream on top and some chocolate syrup.
b. Because they are in different time zones.
c. You need water and sunlight.
d. It's really late! It's midnight.
e. I like whales best of all.

4. Write. Think about these four things, and note your ideas. Then work with a partner. Ask and answer questions.

1. prettiest sea creature
2. funniest sea creature
3. biggest sea creature
4. ugliest sea creature

What's the prettiest sea creature?

It's an octopus!

5. Read and write.

1. You are swimming in the ocean. You feel lots of arms touching your legs. You count them. There are eight of them. It's an ___octopus___ !

2. It's late. The town is very quiet. Everyone is sleeping. The clock makes a sound twelve times. It's _____ !

3. It is early morning. Your room is dark. You are still in bed. Suddenly something comes through your window. It's bright. It's _____ !

4. You are on a boat. Some dolphins are playing in the water! Suddenly you can't see them anymore. What happened? They _____ underwater.

SONG

1 **Match words that rhyme in A and B.** Write all the A words in the song. Then listen to the song to check your answers. TR: 6.2

A	B
motion	sea
~~please~~	ocean
know	seas
me	below
sea	we

Please, _please_ protect the seas.
Put good deeds into _____.
Help save the oceans.

1.
We must protect
the wonders of the seas,
to make a better world
for you and _____ .

2.
When we make a mess,
we can't dump it into the _____ .
Sharks don't want that. Do we?

3.
There are layers in the ocean below.
There are creatures that we don't
_____ . They live deep underwater.
They don't breathe air, but our world is a part of theirs.

2 **Read the song again.** Check T for *True* and F for *False*.

1. We protect the oceans to make a worse world.   T   F
2. The sharks want a clean ocean. We do, too.   T   F
3. We know all the creatures in the sea.   T   F
4. Ocean creatures and people share the same world.   T   F

GRAMMAR 1

Have to, must, can't, and don't

We	**must** / **have to**	keep	the classroom clean.	
You	**can't**	throw	trash on the floor.	can't = can not
	Don't	throw	trash on the floor.	don't = do not

To talk about rules, use *must, have to, can't,* and *don't*.

1 **Look and write.** Complete the sentences.

be	put
fish	~~swim~~
pick up	use

1. You ___can't swim___ at this beach.
2. We _____ our bottles in a recycling bin.
3. You _____ here! The waves are dangerous.
4. We _____ our trash before we go.
5. You _____ your cell phone here.
6. This is a library. You _____ quiet.

2 **Write.** What about you? Make four true sentences.

1. I have to get up at six on weekdays.
2. _____
3. _____
4. _____
5. _____

VOCABULARY 2

1 Look and answer. Check all the objects that are biodegradable.

2 Read. Match the questions and answers.

1. Is this bottle of water biodegradable?
2. People say that there are no fish in this sea. Is that true?
3. Ugh! This sand is black, not yellow. The water is black, too. What happened?
4. Why are our oceans and rivers so dirty?

a. Yes, it is. There was a lot of overfishing here a few years ago.
b. No, it isn't. It's plastic!
c. People throw garbage into the rivers. Then the garbage travels to the sea.
d. There was a big oil spill last year. We are still cleaning up.

3 Write. What can we do to protect the ocean? Write your ideas. Use four words from each list.

oil spill	plastic
garbage	biodegradable
overfishing	

clean up	stop
pick up	throw
put	

_____
_____
_____
_____

82 Unit 6

GRAMMAR 2

Future with *will* and *won't*

| In the future, | people | **will** | live | longer. | won't = will not |
| | we | **won't** | use | paper money. | |

Question					Answer	
Where	**will**	we	live	in the future?	We**'ll** live in very big cities. We **won't** live in small towns.	we'll = we will
	Will	people	live	longer?	Yes, they **will**. No, they **won't**.	

When you aren't 100% sure, use *maybe*.
In the future, will people live longer? Maybe.

1 **Read and write.**

1. ___Will___ people ___live___ under the ocean in the future?
   Yes, they will. There will be underwater cities.

2. ____ children _____ (study at school / 10 years)?
   _____

3. ____ we _____ (go to the movies / the future)?
   _____

2 **Listen.** What do Ken and Misao think? Check how our lives will be different in 20 years. TR: 6.3

	Boy	Girl
1. have a computer in our bodies	✓	✗
2. live in the same house		
3. eat very little food		
4. have water		
5. feel sick		

83

READING

1 Listen and read. TR: 6.4

Weird but true: A shark can grow and lose 30,000 teeth in a lifetime.

Looking for Lunch

It's another busy day in the ocean. All the sea creatures are looking for food. ZAP! A coral polyp catches a small fish as it swims by. It eats the fish. Energy passes from the fish to the polyp. Next, a parrotfish sees the coral polyp. It moves closer. Crrrrrunchhhh! The parrotfish eats the soft parts inside the polyp. Energy moves another link up the food chain. It keeps the parrotfish alive, but not for long! Next, a blacktip reef shark swims by and sees the parrotfish. Its sharp teeth cut the parrotfish. Gulp! The energy that was in the parrotfish is now in the shark.

There are many food chains in the ocean because sea creatures—like people—eat more than one thing. And many animals fight for the same food. For example, some sea turtles eat sea grasses. Surgeonfish do, too. All the chains connect to form a "food web." In this web of life, energy moves from creature to creature. Awesome! We are all connected to the ocean.

2 Check T for True and F for False.

1. Sea creatures get energy when they eat other creatures.   T   F
2. Energy moves from strong creatures to weak creatures.   T   F
3. There is only one food chain in the sea.   T   F
4. A food chain is part of a food web.   T   F

3 **Read and write.** Write the order in which each creature eats the next creature.

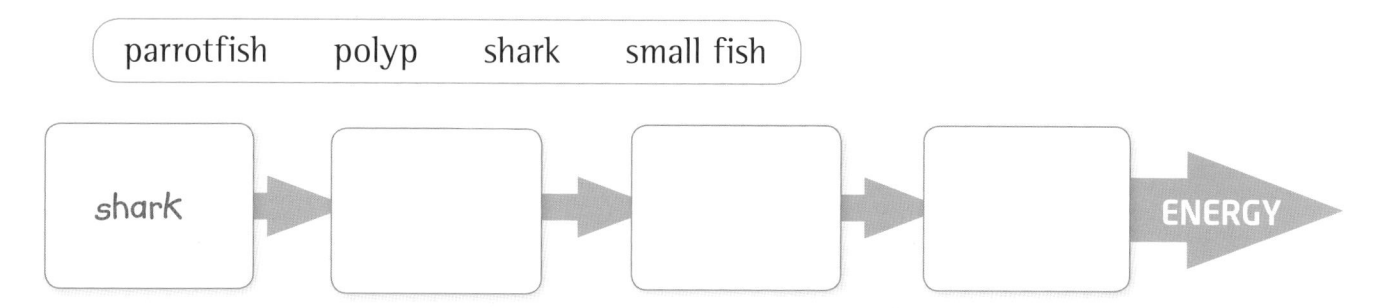

parrotfish   polyp   shark   small fish

shark → ☐ → ☐ → ☐ → ENERGY

4 **Write.** Label the sea creatures. Then work with a partner. Talk about food chains and the food web.

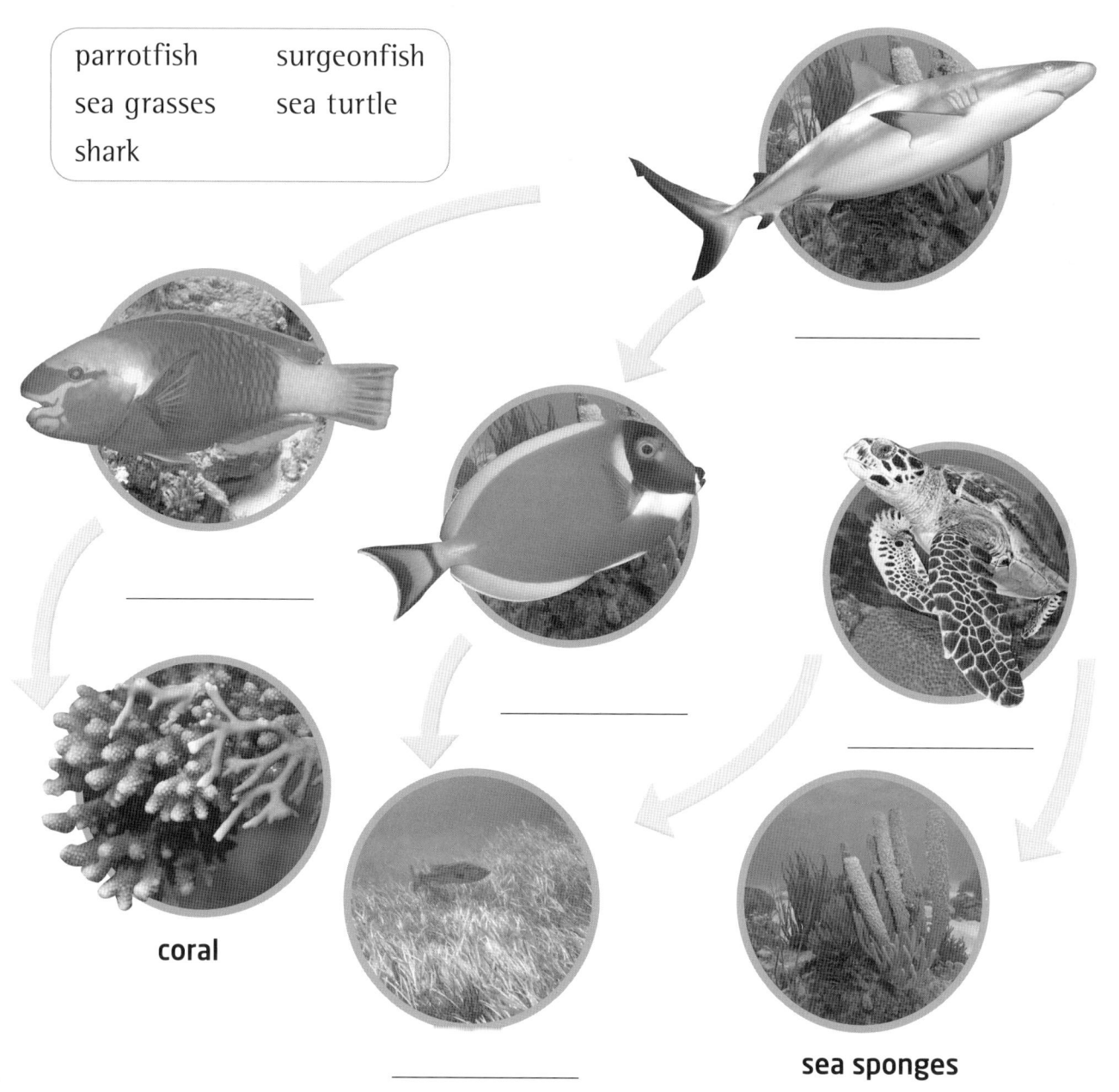

parrotfish   surgeonfish
sea grasses   sea turtle
shark

coral

sea sponges

85

WRITING

1 **Read *Land and Sea Turtles* in your Student's Book.** How did the writer plan her writing? Read the steps.

1. First, the writer chose two things with clear differences to write about. Land and sea turtles have important differences.
2. Next, the writer wrote down ideas about the turtles.
3. After that, she wrote down how land and sea turtles are different.

```
                appearance
                    |
habitats ——— turtles ——— behavior
                    |
              life as a baby
```

land turtle	sea turtle
babies stay on land	babies crawl from land to the water
live in different habitats	live in the ocean
hard, high round shells	soft, flat shells
when afraid, hide in their shells	can't hide in shells, swim fast
dig holes in the ground and sleep all winter	when cold, swim away to warmer waters

4. Then she thought of words and expressions that show contrast:
   but   however   in contrast
5. Finally, she wrote her first version, called a draft, of her writing.

2 **What do you remember about warm and cold corals?** Write information in the chart. Read *Colorful Corals* in your Student's Book if you need help.

Warm Corals	Cold Corals
live in _____	live in _____
need sunlight to grow	don't need sunlight
smaller	larger
eat _____	eat _____
grow quickly	grow slowly

Unit 6

3 Write sentences. Use the chart and *but, however,* and *in contrast*.

1. Warm corals need sunlight to grow. In contrast, cold corals don't need sunlight.
2. _____
3. _____
4. _____
5. _____

4 Circle. Which is the best sentence to begin your writing? Circle the number.

1. We must protect our coral reefs and ocean habitats now.
2. Warm and cold corals are different in several ways.
3. Polyps are small, individual animals that live in water.

5 Now follow steps 2-5 in Activity 1. Write your paragraphs about corals in your notebook.

6 Express yourself. Choose one of the topics below and write two or three paragraphs of contrast. Plan your writing and follow the steps in Activity 1. Write in your notebook.

sharks and dolphins   two family members   oceans and rivers
TV and movies   two vacations   soccer and basketball

87

UNIT 6 REVIEW

1 Write as many sentences as you can. Try to use all the images.

There are many fish in the top layer of the ocean because there is a lot of sunlight.

2 Read and underline the correct words.

So you're going on your first beach clean-up. What do you (1) *have to / must* do? It's easy! You (2) *must / can't* pick up the trash that people left on the beach. But there are some things to remember. First, (3) *can't / don't* forget to wear gloves. If you wear gloves, you (4) *will / won't* cut yourself on the glass. Also, you (5) *will / won't* probably feel thirsty, so it's a good idea to bring water. You (6) *have / must* bring a bottle that you can use again. You (7) *don't / can't* bring soda cans!

3 Read and write. Write four complete sentences about how to clean up a beach.

can't	must
don't	will
have to	won't

Welcome to the Beach Clean-up!

Please follow these rules:
1. Wear comfortable shoes. No sandals.
2. Bring sunscreen: Protect yourself when you protect the ocean.
3. Wear a hat. No umbrellas!
4. Do not pick up dead animals or birds.
5. Do not pick up heavy things. You don't want to hurt your back!

1. You have to wear comfortable shoes. Don't wear sandals.

2. _____

3. _____

4. _____

5. _____

Unit 7
Good Idea!

VOCABULARY 1

1 **Do the puzzle.** Circle the words. Then label the picture.

- battery
- creativity
- electricity
- fail
- idea
- imagination
- invent
- invention
- problem
- solution
- succeed
- try
- useful
- wheel

I	M	A	G	I	N	A	T	I	O	N	K
G	F	R	T	Y	G	B	N	N	V	X	L
B	A	T	T	E	R	Y	X	V	W	W	I
X	I	X	W	L	A	W	H	E	E	L	N
A	L	S	D	E	F	G	H	N	J	K	V
E	F	T	Y	C	C	V	B	T	B	U	E
S	O	L	U	T	I	O	N	K	L	S	N
Z	A	Q	P	R	O	B	L	E	M	E	T
Q	W	E	R	I	D	E	A	T	Y	F	I
M	S	U	C	C	E	E	D	N	T	U	O
B	V	C	R	I	F	V	G	B	R	L	N
C	R	E	A	T	I	V	I	T	Y	D	A
X	C	E	I	Y	U	J	M	I	K	O	L

electricity

90 Unit 7

2 Complete.

> creativity   failing   ideas   imagination   invention
> ~~problem~~   solution   succeed   trying   useful

Do you love science? When you see a __problem__, do you want to find a _____? Do you have the _____ to think up a new _____? If so, perhaps you are one of more than 7 million young people every year who take part in local science fairs.

At these events, young scientists and inventors get together to show the projects they are working on and meet other young people. They also aim to show the judges that their inventions are the best and the most _____!

The winners are able to go on to a week-long international science fair. This science fair lets 1,700 young scientists and inventors from 78 countries share their _____ and show their work to the world.

So what does it take to be a winner? The best young inventors need to be smart. They need _____, too. In addition, they are not afraid of _____. If something doesn't work the first time, they keep _____ different ways until they _____.

3 Write. What about you? Write your answers.

1. Think of the inventions you use every day. Which one is the most useful?

_____

2. Do you use a lot of electricity in your home? How can you use less?

_____

3. Are you a good friend? What do you do when a friend has a problem?

_____

4. What advice do you give a friend who fails at something?

_____

SONG

1 **Write.** Label the inventions. Then listen and write them in the song. TR: 7.1

airplanes _____ _____

_____ _____

Inventions solve problems.

Problems that we used to have are gone!

The _____ and the _____

help to make our world go around!

Inventions are useful,

every day, in every way.

_____, _____, and _____

help to make our world go around.

2 **Write another verse.** Work with a partner.

_____

_____

_____

_____

GRAMMAR 1

Used to for past habits

I		walk	to school.	These days	I ride my bike.
He	**used to**				he takes the bus.
People					they drive.
My family	**didn't use to**	have	a car.	Now	we have one.

Question						Answer	
Where	did	you	**use to**	live?		I **used to** live in Seoul.
	Did	you	**use to**	live	in Seoul?	Yes, I did. / No, I didn't.

You can use *used to* when you talk about things you did regularly in the past but you don't do anymore. Remember to use *use to* in questions with *did* and after *didn't*.

1 **Look and write.** Complete the sentences and questions.

1. How __did__ this family __use to live__ (live)?
2. These people _____ (not / live) in an apartment. They _____ (live) in a house.
3. They _____ (not / buy) meat. They _____ (grow) their own food.
4. This family _____ (sleep) on the floor. They _____ (not / have) beds.
5. ___ these people _____ (travel) by car? No, they _____ (walk).
6. ___ they _____ (use) electricity? No, they _____ (light) a fire.

2 **Write.** Is your family life now different from when you were younger? How?

We used to live in an apartment when I was five. Now we live in a house.

93

VOCABULARY 2

1 **Read.** Circle the best word.

1. This invention, called a "toothpaste squeezer," is easy to _____ ! a. use   b. move
2. First, _____ the toothpaste tube in the squeezer. a. lift   b. put
3. Now _____ the key at the end of the squeezer. a. turn   b. lift
4. The tube _____ and the toothpaste comes out. a. turns   b. moves
5. _____ your toothbrush to your mouth and brush! a. Use   b. Lift

2 **Listen.** Answer the questions. TR: 7.2

1. What does Irma think of this invention?
   _____

2. Why does Daniel think it's silly?
   _____
   _____

3 **Listen again.** Write the order in which you hear these sentences (1-6). TR: 7.3

( ) Why don't you just lift the bottle with your hand and give it to me?

( ) So, I move it across the table to you . . . like this!

( ) Well, now you put the sauce on your fries.

( ) So the wheels turn . . . so what?

(1) Really? How do you use it?

( ) Use your imagination! It's easy!

94   Unit 7

GRAMMAR 2

You for general statements

Question				Answer
What	can	you	do with this phone?	**You** can take nice photos.
How	do		play the game *Head's Up*?	First, **you** choose a topic. Then **you** ...

you = people (in general)

1 **Read.** Check the sentences that are about people in general.

- ✓ 1. How do you pronounce *wheel* in English?
- ○ 2. Please can you show me how to use this?
- ○ 3. What do you think is the best invention ever, Ming?
- ○ 4. I don't know how to play bingo. How do you play it?
- ○ 5. Is this a new toy? What do you do with it?

2 **Play a game.** Listen to the descriptions of inventions. Check the box when you hear the description. Stop when you have three pictures in a line! TR: 7.4

READING

1 Listen and read. TR: 7.5

Trains Make the World Go Round

Stand back! A famous train is coming into the station! It's called the *Shinkansen*, although many people call it the *bullet train* because of its long round nose.

These Japanese trains, invented by Hideo Shima in the early 1960s, are amazing. They're one of the fastest trains in the world. The journey from Tokyo to Nagano used to take three hours. Now, with the bullet train, which travels at 300 kilometers per hour (186 miles per hour), it takes 79 minutes. Bullet trains are always on time (although once it was 42 seconds late!), and they're comfortable. As you sit on the train, you feel like you aren't moving at all. And because they run on electricity, they're very quiet. But don't fall asleep. There is a lot to see. The bullet train travels across 300 bridges, and you can see the wonderful Mount Fuji out the window, too.

In fact, trains are popular in many parts of the world, not just Japan. Every day *billions* of people around the world travel by train, especially in China, India, and Europe. Trains are the fastest way to travel on land, and they're the safest, too (cars and buses are much more dangerous). And although most trains are more expensive than they used to be, trains still make the world go round!

2 Read the text. Check T for *True* or F for *False*.

1. The *Shinkansen* is called the *bullet train* because of its shape. T F
2. Bullet trains are the slowest trains in the world. T F
3. A billion people take the bullet train every day. T F
4. Trains are very popular in Asia and Europe. T F
5. Trains used to be cheaper than they are today. T F

3 **Read and write.** Read about bullet trains again. Match the sentence halves.

1. Bullet trains are very
2. When you are on the train,
3. The trains travel at
4. There are views from
5. They're always

a. on time.
b. hundreds of bridges.
c. quiet.
d. you feel like you aren't moving.
e. around 300 km/h.

4 **Write.** Complete the chart with the opinions about bullet trains.

> There is a lot to see. Bullet trains are very quiet. They're comfortable.
> They're always on time. ~~They're very fast.~~

Opinion	Supporting facts
1. They're very fast.	The trains travel at around 300 km/h.
2.	The train was only late once. It ran 42 seconds late!
3.	When you are on the train, you feel like you aren't moving.
4.	They run on electricity, which means they make little noise.
5.	There are views from hundreds of bridges.

Weird but true: The original bullet trains, the 0 Series, which stopped running in 2008, made enough trips to circle the Earth 30,000 times.

5 **Write.** Imagine you took the bullet train. Make notes in your notebook about the trip. Then work with a partner. Do a role-play. Take turns.

Student A - you took the bullet train.

Student B - ask your partner about the trip.

WRITING

1 **Read *A Good Idea* in your Student's Book.** How did the writer plan her writing? Read the steps.

1. First, the writer chose an invention that she likes: sticky notes.

2. Next, she read about sticky notes. She listed her opinions and the facts that she learned. (A fact is a piece of true information, for example, a date, an event, or a name. We use facts to support our opinions.) She used a chart to do this.

Complete the chart.

Opinions	Supporting facts
a. They're a really good idea and they're easy to use.	You lift the paper off, write a note, and stick it on your notebook or on your computer. And they come off easily.
b. They're popular.	
c. _____	They have two inventors. In 1970, Spencer Silver invented the glue. In 1974, Arthur Fry found a way to use the glue (it was an accident!).

3. Next, the writer thought of words and expressions that show opinions:

(In my opinion   I think   I believe)

4. Then she used her chart and some expressions of opinion.

Write three examples of opinions that you find in her paragraphs.

In my opinion, sticky notes are a great invention.

_____

_____

5. Finally, she wrote the first version, called a draft, of her writing.

2 **Choose another invention.** What do you like about it? What facts can you use to support your opinions? Complete the chart.

Opinions	Supporting facts

3 **Now follow steps 2-5 in Activity 1.** Write about your invention in your notebook.

4 **Write.** Choose one of the topics below and write two or three paragraphs of fact and opinion. Plan your writing and follow the steps in Activity 1. Write in your notebook. Check that your writing has opinions and that there is a fact to support each opinion.

a useful school subject
your favorite actor
pollution in oceans and rivers

TV and movies
your favorite book or writer
big families and small families

UNIT 7 REVIEW

1 **Read.** Underline the correct word.

In 1906 Frank Fleer *lifted / tried* to make bubble gum, but it didn't taste good and stuck to everything! No one bought his *invention / wheel* called "Blibber-Blubber" and Fleer *failed / succeeded*. Twenty years later, Fleer's employee Walter Diemer had a better *idea / problem*. He *put / turned* latex from trees in his bubble gum. Diemer *succeeded / lifted*! He *turned / invented* "Double Bubble." However, there was a *solution / problem*: kids didn't know how to *use / put* bubble gum! The Fleer Company quickly found a *wheel / solution*: they went to cities and showed people how to blow bubbles! You can do anything with some *electricity / imagination* and *creativity / a battery*.

2 **Listen.** Listen to the sounds. Write the verbs in the correct column. TR: 7.6

failed	succeeded
invented	tried
lifted	turned
moved	used

failed _____   _invented_ _____

3 **Match.** Make true sentences.

Frank Fleer — invented — people how to blow bubbles.
Fleer's gum — succeeded — to make bubble gum.
Walter Diemer — showed — "Double Bubble."
Diemer's gum — tried — because no one bought it.
The Fleer Company — failed — because it used latex.

4 **Write.** Write notes on what an umbrella is and how it works. Then work with a partner. Imagine your friend doesn't know what an umbrella is. Explain it.

5 **Write.** Think of your three favorite inventions. Describe them in your notebook. Then compare your answers with a partner.

6 **Look, read, and write.** Complete the paragraph with *used to* or *didn't use to*.

The Hobby Horse

1. People _____ *ride* this bicycle; they used to walk with it and move the handlebars! Most people _____ walk with it in gardens and parks.
2. Women _____ use bikes in those days. Only men used the Hobby Horse.
3. It _____ be difficult to lift or move. It was heavy because it was made of wood.

The High Wheel Bicycle

1. People _____ ride this bicycle, but it wasn't easy! The seat was very high, and the front wheel was very big.
2. People often _____ fall off because the back wheel _____ turn very easily.
3. The pedals were on the front wheel, so it _____ be difficult to move them.

7 **Write.** Make questions with *did . . . use to* or *used to*. Then discuss the answers with a partner.

1. Why / people / fall off / the High Wheel Bicycle?

   Why did people use to fall off the High Wheel Bicycle?

2. Where / people / use / the Hobby Horse?

   _____

3. Which parts of / the Hobby Horse / move or turn?

   _____

Unit 8
That's Really Interesting!

VOCABULARY 1

1 Do a puzzle. Find the words and the secret message!

LEANO	A L O N E (5)
REGTOHTE	_ _ _ _ _ _ _ _
PTNISO	_ _ _ (14) _ (9) _ _
MEETCPO	_ _ _ (1) _ _ _ _
SEENRC	_ _ (8) _ _ _
ROTCNRELLO	_ _ _ _ _ (6) _ _ _ _
JYOEN	_ (10) _ _ (7) _
EACIRTEV	_ _ _ (4) _ _ _ _
YOBHB	_ _ (11) _ (12)
LETCLCO	_ _ _ (13) _ (3) _ _
REOCS	_ _ _ (15) _
TEREPAOCO	_ _ _ _ _ _ _ _ _
RAAATV	_ _ _ _ (2) _

Word bank:
- ~~alone~~
- avatar
- collect
- compete
- controller
- cooperate
- creative
- enjoy
- hobby
- points
- score
- screen
- together

Secret message:
W _ (1) | _ _ _ L _ _ _ (2-7) | _ _ _ _ _ (8-12) | _ _ F (13-15)

102 Unit 8

2 Look and write. Label the pictures. Use words from Activity 1.

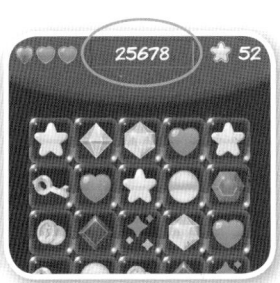

_____ _____ _____ _____

3 Read and write. Complete the sentences.

alone	cooperate	score
avatar	~~enjoy~~	screen
compete	points	together

Do you want to play video games, but you don't know where to start? That's not surprising because there are a lot of games to choose from!

There are many video games for one person, if you __enjoy__ doing things _____. You can try to solve a puzzle or test how much you know about a subject. You get _____ for every correct answer, and try to beat your own _____ next time.

But you may find it more fun to play with friends. If you like working _____, some games need you to _____ with another person. If you want to try to beat someone at a game, choose a game where you _____ with each other. You will each need to choose an _____—a figure to represent you in the game. Some games even let you design your own, so you can decide how you want to look on the _____. That's fun!

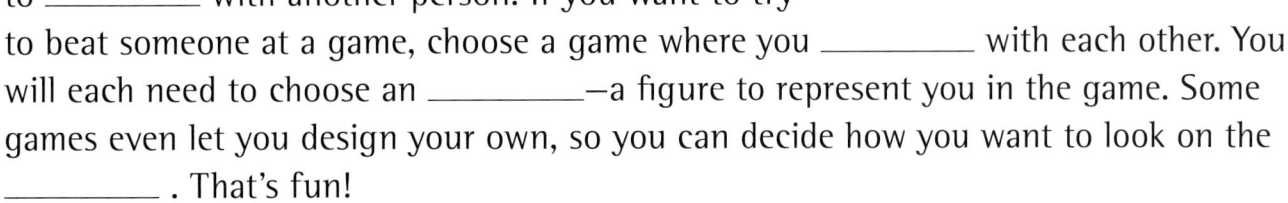

4 Write. What about you? Write about yourself.

1. What hobby or hobbies do you have?

   _____

2. What is the most creative activity that you did recently?

   _____

SONG

1 **Listen to the song.** Match the sentence halves. TR: 8.1

1. The boy who has the highest score
2. The girl who collects a fossil
3. I collect stuffed animals
4. The girl who reads about dinosaurs
5. I like to talk about my hobby

because I think they're sweet.
can see them in her dreams.
on my new cell phone.
wins the video game.
wants to learn its name.

2 **Describe the pictures.** Use sentences from Activity 1. Then pick another sentence from Activity 1 and draw it in the box. Describe it below.

I got the most points! I won!

What's this called?

I'm watching sea turtles tomorrow.

a. The boy who has the highest score wins the video game.

b. _____

c. _____

d. _____

3 **Listen and write.** Listen to the chorus. Cross out the extra words. Then write your own chorus with a partner. TR: 8.2

What's your favorite hobby?
What do you often like to do?
What's your friend's hobby?
I have a cool hobby, too.

104 Unit 8

GRAMMAR 1

Describing people with *who*

I have <u>a friend</u>.	<u>She</u> collects coins.
I have a friend **who** collects coins.	
Nico has <u>two sisters</u>.	<u>They</u> play soccer.
Nico has two sisters **who** play soccer.	
<u>The boy</u> is friendly.	<u>He</u> sits next to me.
The boy **who** sits next to me is friendly.	
<u>The people</u> are French.	<u>They</u> live next door.
The people **who** live next door are French.	

You can use *who* to combine two sentences and describe or define the person you're talking about.

1 Look and listen. Look at the photos. Why might people choose these things as their avatars? Listen and write the number (1–5). TR: 8.3

a.   b.   c.   d.   e.

2 Read and write. Read the sentences about pictures a–e. Choose the best expression. Add *who*.

> is creative
> ride horses
> loves teddy bears
> must have the highest score
> enjoy sports

a. I like this photo. It's great for people ___who enjoy sports___.

b. This is a wonderful choice for people _____ for a hobby.

c. This is great for my friend _____. She loves to take photos of nature, too.

d. This is a good choice for my sister. She is a person _____.

e. Mario should choose this. He is someone _____!

3 Read clues and write. Work with a partner. Student 1, go to page 127. Student 2, go to page 130. Complete the puzzle.

105

VOCABULARY 2

1 Look and write. Label the objects in the science museum store.

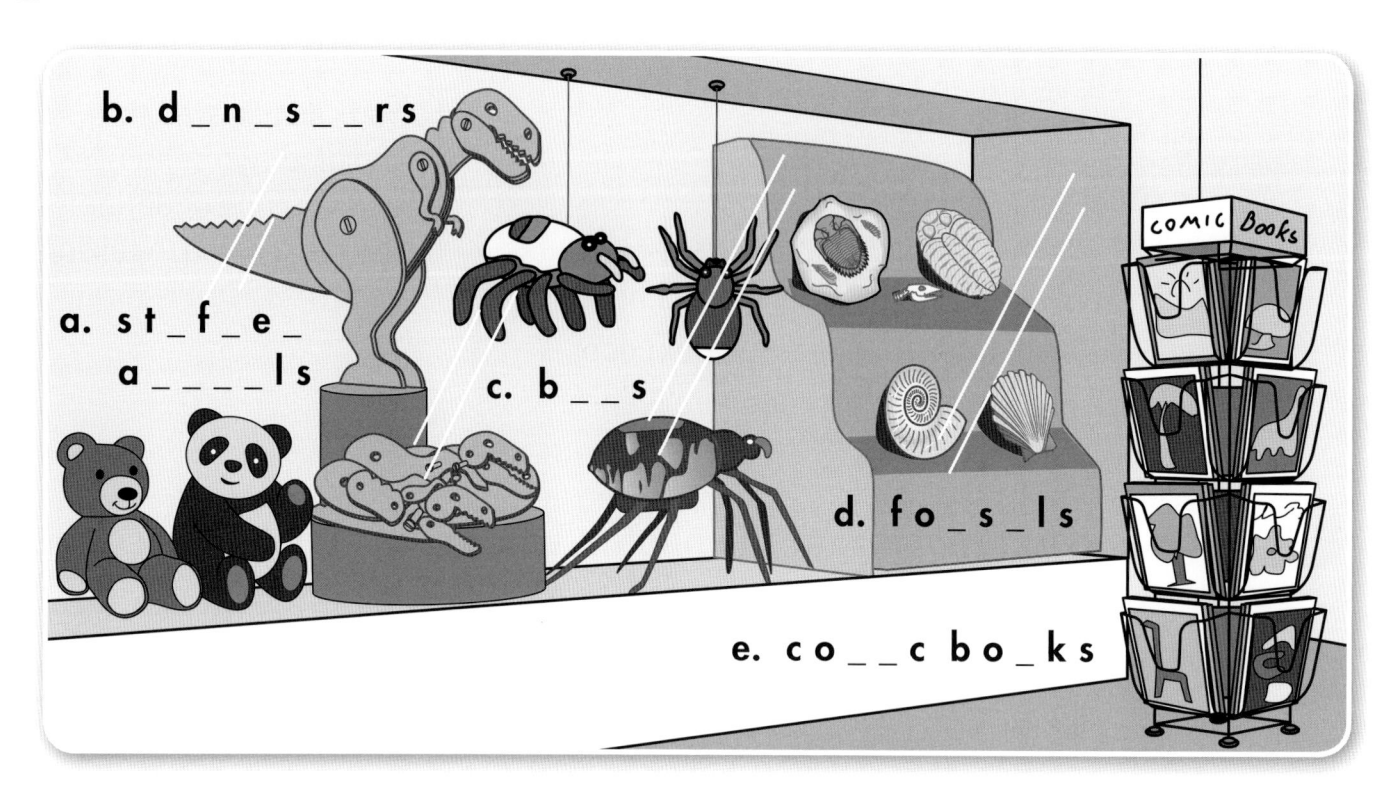

a. st_f_e_ a____ls
b. d_n_s__rs
c. b__s
d. fo_s_ls
e. co___c bo_ks

2 Listen. Number the order that Irma talks about these toys (1–5). **TR: 8.4**

○ bugs   ○ dinosaurs   ○ stuffed animals

○ comic books   ○ fossils

3 Listen again. Underline. **TR: 8.5**

1. The *stuffed animals / bugs* are cute, but her brother is a bit old for them.

2. Irma thinks that the *fossils / dinosaurs* are old-fashioned.

3. The *stuffed animals / bugs* move if you put batteries in them.

4. The *bugs / dinosaurs* are good for her brother because he's creative.

5. Irma buys the *fossils / comic books* for her brother because they are the easiest.

GRAMMAR 2

Direct and indirect objects

Jason	gave	**me**	the comic book.			Object pronouns: me, you, her, him, us, them
Jason	gave		the comic book	**to**	**me**.	
Our teacher	made	**us**	a cake.			
Our teacher	made		a cake	**for**	**us**.	

The two sentences mean the same thing.
Jason gave <u>me</u> <u>the comic book</u>. = Jason gave <u>the comic book</u> **to** <u>me</u>.
With *make* and *buy*, use *for*: Our teacher made / bought a cake **for** us.

1 **Look at pictures 1–4.** Underline the correct verb.

1. Last week we had to <u>make</u> / *buy* / *give* a poster for two classmates.
2. So we *told* / *made* / *sold* Jaime and Delia a bug poster.
3. Later we *showed* / *sold* / *wrote* the teacher our work. She liked it.
4. After that, Jaime and Delia *sold* / *told* / *gave* us a wonderful fossil poster.

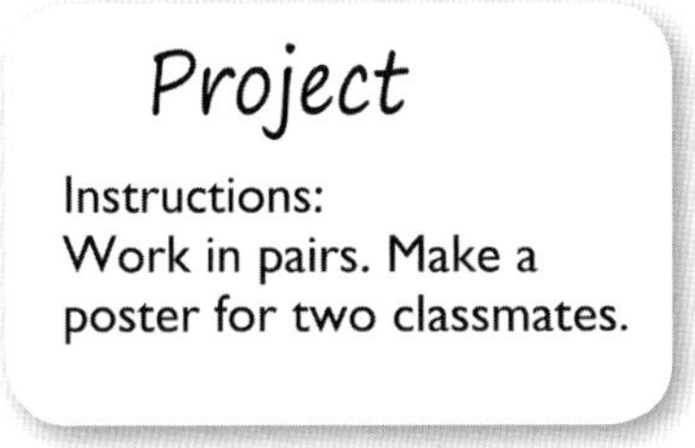

2 **Write.** Write the sentences from Activity 1 in a different way.

<u>Last week we had to make two classmates a poster.</u>

READING

1 Listen and read. TR: 8.6

Video Games: Then and Now

Today video games are played by boys, girls, women, and men of all ages around the world. But how did video games start?

1. One of the first video games ever invented, in 1958, was a tennis game. Players used a controller to hit a ball over a net on a small screen. It was slow and simple compared with today's video games.

2. Video games first became popular in the 1970s. To play, the gamers—mostly young men—went to video arcades. Arcades were like shopping malls full of machines. This changed in 1972, with the invention of the first home video game. Gamers could plug a game console into their home TV. Soon people wanted small portable games, too. The first successful handheld game came out in 1989. After that, people could play games almost anywhere.

3. In the 1990s, two inventions changed gaming forever: cell phones and the internet. In 1994, the first very popular multiplayer game was released. Gamers could play online with more than one person at the same time, cooperating and competing. The game attracted millions of players.

4. Game consoles developed fast in the 2000s, with faster games and better pictures and sound. In 2006, a new console was aimed at more active users. The controller detected movement in all directions, and users had to get up and move around. Sports such as virtual tennis, baseball, and golf became popular.

5. In the 2010s, virtual reality headsets were developed. Players wear these on their heads. What the player sees and hears is controlled by the headset. Gamers need a fast and powerful computer.

108 Unit 8

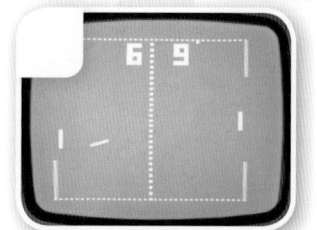

2 Read the text again. Check T for *True* and F for *False*.

1. In the 1970s, mostly young men went to video arcades.   T   F
2. Arcades were in shopping malls.   T   F
3. People wanted to be able to play video games everywhere.   T   F
4. You don't need a computer to play virtual reality games.   T   F

3 Read the text again. Look at the photos. Write the paragraph number next to each photo.

4 Read. Complete the chart. Add your ideas for the future. Then work with a partner and discuss your ideas.

Video games		
When?	**What?**	**Description**
1958		Slow and simple
1972	The first home video game	
1994	Online multiplayer game	
2006		Players moved around and could even play sports
2010s	Virtual reality headsets	
The future		

109

WRITING

1 **Read *Fun with Paper* in your Student's Book.** How did the writer plan her writing? Read the steps.

1. First, the writer chose a hobby to write about. Write the name of the hobby. _____

2. Next, the writer wrote down questions about her hobby to help her think about the topic. She used a word map.

```
            Where is it from?
                  |
What can you make? — hobby — What is it?
                  |
            How do you do it?
```

3. After researching the answers, she checked her ideas. Are there any words that the reader may not know? Do any ideas need examples? She decided that, to help the reader understand her explanation, she needed to give *one definition* and *two examples*.

   a. Which word did she define for us? _____

   b. What is an example of a "simple" shape? _____

   c. What is an example of a "difficult" shape? _____

4. Then she chose words and expressions that show examples. Underline the two that she used.

   such as   like   for example

5. Next she planned the introduction. Compare her introduction with the second introduction below (from: *Hide and Seek* on page 46). What do they have in common?

   a. The Japanese invented origami in the 17th century, and now it is popular everywhere in the world.

   b. *Geocaching* is a fun outdoor hobby. It's like a game of hide and seek, with the hiders leaving clues for the seekers to find.

6. Finally, she wrote the first version, called a draft, of her writing.

110   Unit 8

2 **Now choose a hobby.** Look at Activity 2 in your Student's Book. Follow steps 1-6 in Activity 1. Write your explanation in your notebook.

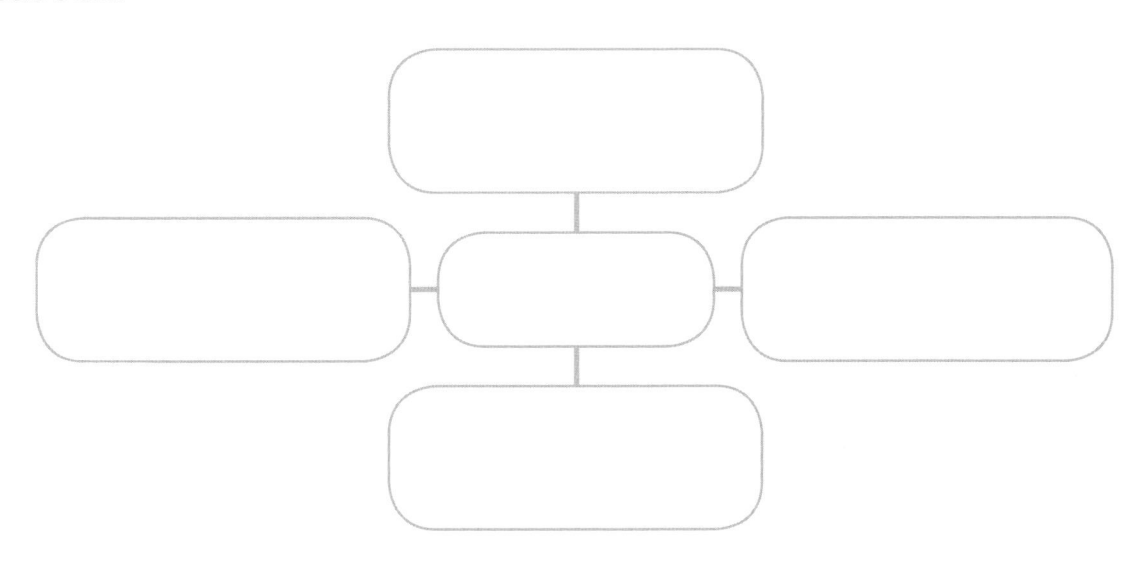

3 **Write.** Choose one of the topics below and write an explanation. Give some examples. Define words that the reader may not know. Plan your writing and follow the steps in Activity 1. Write your new paragraph in your notebook.

A toy you like

One of your video games

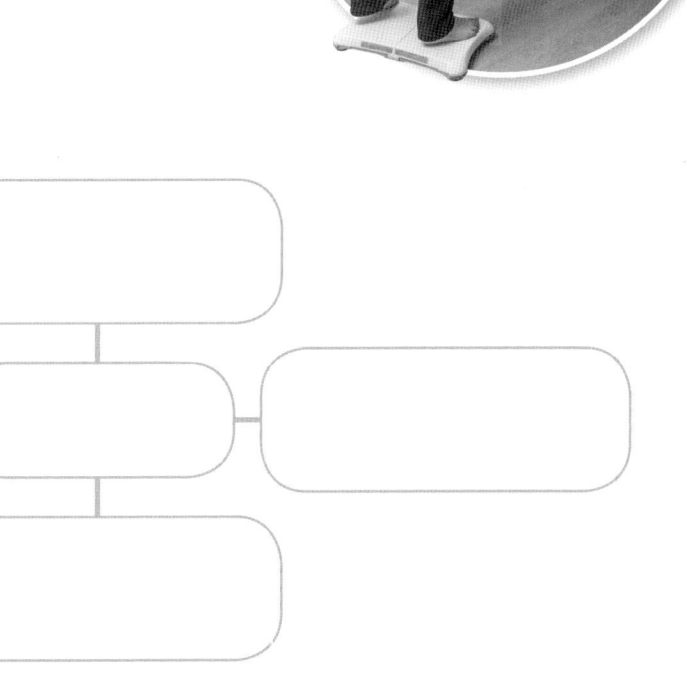

A sport you enjoy

UNIT 8 REVIEW

1 Read and write. Read the description of the video game. Describe it.

> avatar   collect   controllers   cooperate
> points   score   screen

In this cool game, players can compete or _____. First, choose your _____. Then watch the _____ – dinosaurs are everywhere today. Now try to _____ as many dinosaurs as you can. But remember, if you get a slow dinosaur, you win just two _____. So, for a higher _____ try to get faster dinosaurs. There are only two _____ but four people can play in a cooperative game. Enjoy!

A DAY WITH DINOSAURS

- Avatars for children aged 10–14.
- Players compete to collect dinosaurs. More points for some dinosaurs.
- Watch dinosaurs move on screen. Hear the noise!
- Two controllers for players. Cooperative games also possible.

2 Read. Match the questions and answers.

1. What new hobby do you want to try? _____
2. Do you do anything creative? _____
3. Do you prefer to spend time together with other people or alone? _____
4. Do you like to compete in sports? _____
5. Did you use to collect many things when you were younger? _____

a. Not really. I sometimes play tennis, but I never keep score.
b. A musical group must be really amazing! I want to try that.
c. Well, sometimes I paint or draw. And I often take photos.
d. Sure. I used to have all kinds of things: pens, fossils, and bugs!
e. I enjoy both. But I usually do things by myself.

3 Write. Read the questions in Activity 2 again. Write answers that are true for you. Then work with a partner. Take turns to ask and answer.

4. Read the messages. Complete the sentences with *who*.

Message 1: I'm a ten-year-old boy who wants a hobby because I'm bored. Please don't tell me to do sports. I don't really like sports. Also, I need something that I can do alone.

Message 2: I have hundreds of comic books, and my mom told me to throw some away. I want to send them to a place where other people can read them. Do you have any ideas?

Message 3: I have a young daughter who collects stuffed toys. She has more than thirty, and she wants more. I want to buy more for her, but they are very expensive. What can I do?

1. boy / need a hobby / do not like sports.

   <u>The boy who needs a hobby doesn't like sports.</u>

2. boy / be ten years old / want a hobby.

   _____

3. girl / enjoy comic books / have hundreds of them.

   _____

4. girl / have too many comic books / do not want to put them in the trash.

   _____

5. young girl / collect stuffed toys / want more toys.

   _____

6. mom / wrote the message / think stuffed toys are expensive.

   _____

Unit 9
The Science of Fun

VOCABULARY 1

1 Do the puzzle.

A	R	S	Z	F	O	R	C	E	R	W	V
F	A	L	L	K	R	T	H	R	N	Q	P
O	V	E	R	T	E	O	D	C	X	B	N
R	Q	B	R	Z	M	R	S	R	W	A	F
W	H	N	T	Z	A	V	P	U	L	L	R
A	H	T	M	W	S	Y	I	B	K	A	I
R	S	N	K	D	O	W	N	O	J	N	C
D	K	C	P	J	C	O	N	N	E	C	T
J	A	Z	U	I	R	F	S	A	V	E	I
B	T	J	S	W	I	N	G	K	Y	T	O
A	E	W	H	B	Z	H	A	P	P	E	N
W	R	F	E	N	Q	M	X	E	C	Z	O

~~backward~~   happen
balance   over
connect   pull
down   push
fall   rub
force   skater
forward   spin
friction   swing

2 Look and write. Label the pictures *push* or *pull*.

1. _____
2. _____ 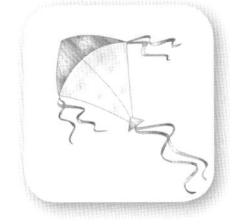
3. _____ 
4. _____ 
5. _____ 
6. _____ 

114   Unit 9

3 Read. Complete the paragraphs. Can you guess who is speaking? Underline.

> balance   connects   down   ~~force~~   forward   friction   over   push   rub

A. "I use ____force____. To move, I push _____ on one of the pedals. The wheels turn, and I move. To stop, I use the brake. The brake _____ with the wheels. The brakes and the four wheels _____ together. When they rub together like this, there is _____."

Who am I? I'm a *cyclist / car driver / skateboarder.*

B. "To move, I _____ on the ground. The push moves me _____. The wheels turn, and I move. Sometimes I go fast, but I don't fall _____ because I know how to balance! To _____, I stand and move my arms in the air."

Who am I? I'm a *cyclist / car driver / skateboarder.*

4 Write. Write about each picture. Describe how they move.

1. _____

2. _____

3. _____

SONG

1 Find four pairs that rhyme.

A	B
you	walk
force	groove
around	do
move	ground
fall	course
work	feel

(you — do)

2 Listen and write the rhyming pairs in the song. TR: 9.1

Push it, pull it, push it, pull it, push, pull. Push, pull, push, pull! Watch it go!

If you spin _____, and around and around and around,
what you feel is _____.
If you fall down, down, down, down, down to the _____,
that's gravity, of _____.

I'm on the _____.
I'm in the _____.
It's amazing what you can do
when you let force _____ the work for you!

The more _____ push, the faster some things go.
When you spin around, the force comes and goes.

3 Circle the correct meaning of each expression.

1. Let force do the work for you!
   - (a.) Force can help you.
   - b. You should work harder.
2. I'm in the groove.
   - a. I want to move.
   - b. I feel happy.
3. I'm on the move.
   - a. I'm moving.
   - b. I'm sitting down.

116 Unit 9

GRAMMAR 1

Cause and effect with double comparatives

The more	she goes up on the seesaw,	the more	he goes down.
The more	you study,	the more	you learn.
The more	you push the swing,	the higher	it goes.
The more	he practices English,	the better	he speaks.

In each sentence, the first action causes the second action.
***The more** she goes up on the seesaw, **the more** he goes down*.
       first action   second action

1 **Read.** Match the sentence halves.

1. You should work hard in school because ____
2. It is important to brush your teeth because ____
3. We walk our dogs often because ____
4. We should try again if we fail because ____
5. We must not pollute the ocean because ____

a. the harder we try, the more we succeed.
b. the harder you study, the more you learn.
c. the dirtier it gets, the faster creatures disappear.
d. the more they walk, the healthier they will be.
e. the better you take care of them, the less you have to see the dentist.

2 **Complete the sentences.** What happens when the boy pushes the merry-go-round?

1. _The more he pushes it_ (he / push / it),
   the faster it turns (fast / it / turn).
2. _____ (fast / it / go),
   _____ (the children / laugh).
3. _____ (funny / it / is),
   _____ (hard / he / push it).
4. _____ (quick / it / spin),
   _____ (dizzy / they / feel).
5. _____ (bad / they / feel),
   _____ (they / scream STOP)!

117

VOCABULARY 2

1 **Read.** Read the clues and write the answer.

> away from   backward   center   direction   friction   toward

1. You are in the park. Some bugs are moving near the tree. Suddenly you can't see them anymore. They disappeared. Which _____ did they go in? Up the tree!
2. You feel sad. You're going to an adventure camp for two weeks. You won't be with your family. You'll be _____ your friends, too. ☹
3. You are asleep and dreaming. In your dream, there is a big monster with two green heads. You're very scared because it is coming _____ you!
4. You buy a candy bar with strawberry filling. On the outside, it is brown. You eat it. In the _____, it is soft and red.

2 **Listen and look.** Check T for *True* or F for *False*. TR: 9.2

1. Gravity is a force. (T✓) (F)
2. Gravity pulls things down. (T) (F)
3. Gravity pulls things toward the center of the earth. (T) (F)
4. Gravity pushes the sun away from us. (T) (F)
5. Ming thinks gravity is boring. (T) (F)

3 **Listen again.** Complete the dialogue. TR: 9.3

Ming: Mrs. Li, can you please explain something?

Mrs. Li: Sure. How can I help you, Ming?

Ming: I still don't understand _gravity_.

Mrs. Li: OK, when you fall over, what _____? You fall down on the ground. That's the _____ of gravity pulling you.

Ming: So gravity _____ everything *down*, right?

Mrs. Li: Not exactly. Gravity doesn't pull things _____. Gravity doesn't pull the sun down to earth, for example! So, what does _____ do?

Ming: Does it pull things _____ the earth?

Mrs. Li: Yes, that's right, Ming! So if you _____, gravity pulls you toward the _____ of the earth.

GRAMMAR 2

Definitions with *which*

Gravity is <u>the force</u>.	<u>It</u> pulls you toward Earth.
Gravity is the force **which** pulls you toward Earth.	
A carnivore is <u>an animal</u>.	<u>It</u> eats meat.
A carnivore is an animal **which** eats meat.	
Skates are special <u>shoes</u>.	You wear <u>them</u> to go skating.
Skates are special shoes **which** you wear to go skating.	
Honey is a sweet <u>food</u>.	Bees make <u>it</u>.
Honey is a sweet food **which** bees make.	

You can use *which* in a sentence to give definitions.

1 Listen and write. Write the clues you hear in the quiz. Then listen again and write the correct answers. **TR: 9.4**

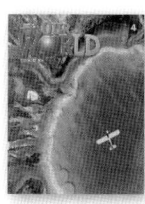

Clues   Answers
1. It's a useful subject _____   _____
2. It's something _____   _____
3. It's a vegetable _____   _____

2 Write. Write clues. Then guess two possible answers.

1. This / a machine with wheels / ride in the park.   <u>a bicycle</u>
   <u>This is a machine with wheels which we ride in the park.</u>   a skateboard

2. It / something / pull.   _____
   _____   _____

3. This / a force / happens / when we move.   _____
   _____   _____

4. This / a popular sport / play / with a ball.   _____
   _____   _____

5. This / an invention / changed our lives.   _____
   _____   _____

6. It / a thing / people / collect for a hobby.   _____
   _____   _____

READING

1 **Listen and read.** TR: 9.5

The Science of Skateboarding

Skateboards are much more than just four wheels connected to a piece of wood. Let's look at the science of the fun! To understand more, we need to study three important parts of the skateboard: the deck, the truck, and the wheels.

The *deck* is the board. It is usually made of maple wood, which is very strong but can bend, too. Modern skateboard decks have curves at the "nose" (the front) and the "tail" (the back). After you push and the wheels start turning, you should put your feet near the curves. They help you balance. Now the skateboard is moving, but you need to control the direction! The *truck*, connected to all the wheels and the deck, helps you control the deck. When you lean to the right, the truck makes the deck turn right. If you lean left, the skateboard turns left. Now what about skateboard *wheels*? Wheels do more than just move the board. They become flatter when you push down on them. And after you stop pushing down, they become round again.

All three parts of the skateboard are important. So if you want to have fun, check that everything works before you go skateboarding! And don't forget your helmet, knee pads, and elbow pads!

2 **Read the text again.** Check T for *True* and F for *False*.

1. To balance, you should stand with your feet near the curves.   T   F
2. The truck helps you control which direction you travel in.   T   F
3. Wheels just move the board.   T   F
4. When you push down on the wheels, they are still round.   T   F
5. Always check that the parts are working before you go skateboarding.   T   F

3 Read and write. Label the parts of a skateboard.

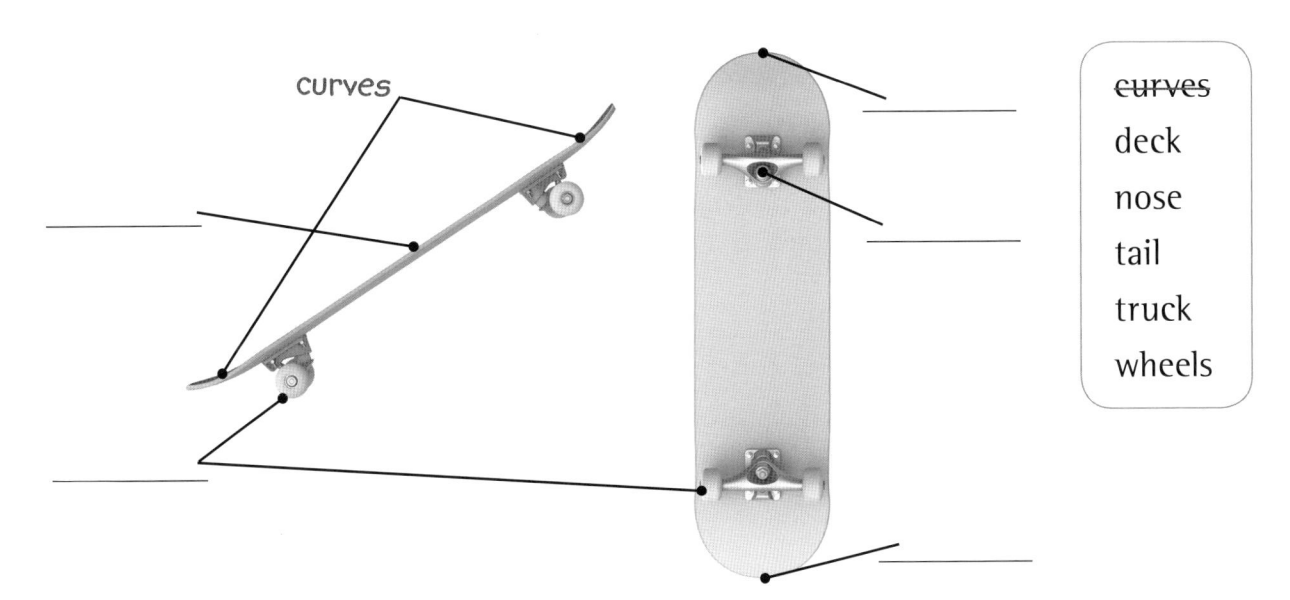

curves

~~curves~~
deck
nose
tail
truck
wheels

A dog called Tillman can skateboard. He moves 100 m (328 feet) in just 19.68 seconds and always chews the wheels before he begins.

4 Read and complete the chart.

Check that your skateboard is working.   You can control the direction.
There are curves on the deck.   It bends, and it is very strong.

CAUSE	EFFECT
1. The deck is made of maple wood.	
2. _____	You can balance more easily.
3. The truck is connected to the wheels.	
4. _____	You won't have an accident.

5 Write. In your notebook, write three sentences about how a skateboard works. Then discuss with a partner.

curve   truck
deck   wheels
direction

balance   lean
bend   move along
connect   put
control   turn

121

WRITING

1 **Read the cause and effect writing in your Student's Book.**
How did the writer plan her writing? Read the steps.

1. First, the writer chose a game that has a variety of movements and that involves cause and effect. Tetherball has many cause-and-effect movements.

2. Next, the writer wrote down a description of the game: the rules, what the players do, typical movements, and her own opinion. She used a word map.

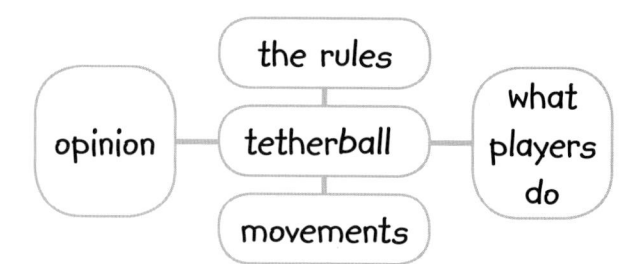

   Which parts of the map do these sentences belong to?
   1. Two people play the game. One person hits the ball to the right. The other person hits it to the left. _____
   2. You hit the ball so that it turns around the pole. _____
   3. Tetherball looks easy. But it isn't. _____

3. After making notes about tetherball, she wrote down some common causes and effects in the game. She used a cause and effect chart to do this.

Cause	Effect
The rope is connected to a pole.	The ball doesn't fly away.
You hit the ball.	It turns around the pole.
When I hit the ball, it flew around in a big circle.	It was easy for my brother to hit it!
When he hit the ball, it went fast and high.	He won every game!

4. Then she thought of words and expressions that show cause and effect:

   (so that   so   as a result)

   Which words or expressions did she use to connect cause and effect sentences?

5. Finally, she wrote the first version, called a draft, of her writing.

2 **Look at Activity 2 in your Student's Book.** Follow steps 1-5 in Activity 1. Plan your paragraph about a game or activity. Use the word map below. Draw a cause and effect chart in your notebook.

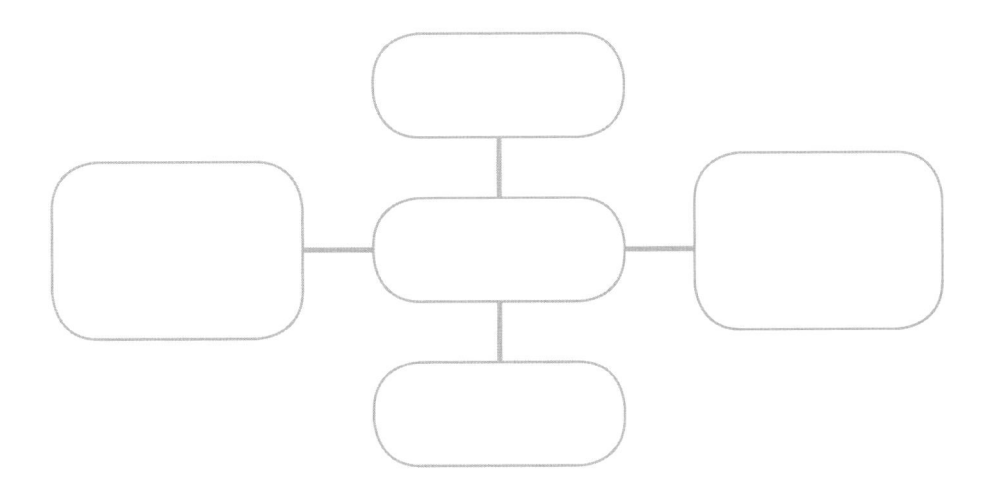

3 **Write cause and effect sentences.** Use the information in your cause and effect chart and connect them with *because, as, so, so that,* and *as a result.* Then write your paragraph in your notebook.

1. When you go on a roller coaster, you have to use a safety bar so that you don't fall out.

2. _____

3. _____

4. _____

4 **Write.** Choose one of the topics below and write two or three paragraphs of cause and effect. Plan your writing and follow the steps in Activity 1. Write in your notebook.

(first-aid kits   hobbies and sports   ocean pollution)

UNIT 9 REVIEW

1 **Look and read.** Choose the correct answer.

1. The car is traveling *toward* / *away from* the zoo.
2. The truck is traveling *toward* / *away from* the mall.
3. The woman in the playground is *pushing* / *pulling* a girl on the swing.
4. The children in the playground are *rubbing* / *spinning* on the merry-go-round.
5. The girl on the bicycle is moving *forward* / *backward*. She is *pushing* / *pulling* the boy who is *falling over* / *balancing* on the skateboard. That's dangerous.
6. They're very silly. A serious accident could *connect* / *happen*.

2 **Do the puzzle.**

a = across
d = down

Everyone was busy having fun. Some children <2a> around on the merry-go-round. A mom <8a> her daughter on the swings. And a girl on a bicycle <5d> her friend, who <7a> on a skateboard behind her. But suddenly something bad <4a>. The girl saw a car coming. When her brakes <6d> with the wheels, she stopped, but her friend wasn't paying attention and he <3d> off his skateboard. Luckily no one was hurt, but the car driver was very angry. The boy got up and <1d> his head. "We're really sorry," he said. "It was silly and dangerous."

3. Look, read, and write. Rewrite the sentences so that they have the same meaning. Then guess the objects!

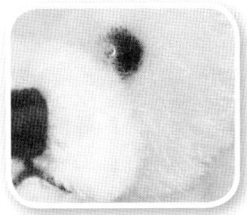

1. It is round. We take it to the beach.
   It is something round which we take to the beach.   a beach ball

2. They are soft. Some people collect them.
   _____   _____

3. It is a classroom object. We rub it on paper.
   _____   _____

4. It is a kind of food. It's cold and tasty!
   _____   _____

5. They are pretty things. You find them in your garden.
   _____   _____

4. Read and complete the clues.

(bigger   faster   ~~higher~~   softer   younger)

1. The more air it has inside it, the ___higher___ the ball bounces.
2. The _____ the person, the more popular this toy is.
3. The harder you rub the eraser, the _____ your words disappear.
4. The longer you leave ice cream in the sun, the _____ it gets.
5. The more you water flowers, the _____ they grow.

5. Write. What about you? Make three true sentences.

1. _The earlier I get up_ (early / get up), _the more time I have to enjoy the day._
2. _____ (happy / feel), _____
3. _____ (late / go to bed), _____
4. _____ (practice / sports), _____

6. Play a game. Work in a small group. Go to page 128.

Unit 8 Student 1, use with Activity 3 on page 105.

3 Complete the puzzle.

A. Look at your words. Give clues to your partner.

B. Listen to your partner's clues and write the words.

1. fast
3. neighbors
4. friend
9. athlete
11. short
12. creative
14. handsome
15. singer
17. teacher

Number 1 across: someone who is not slow

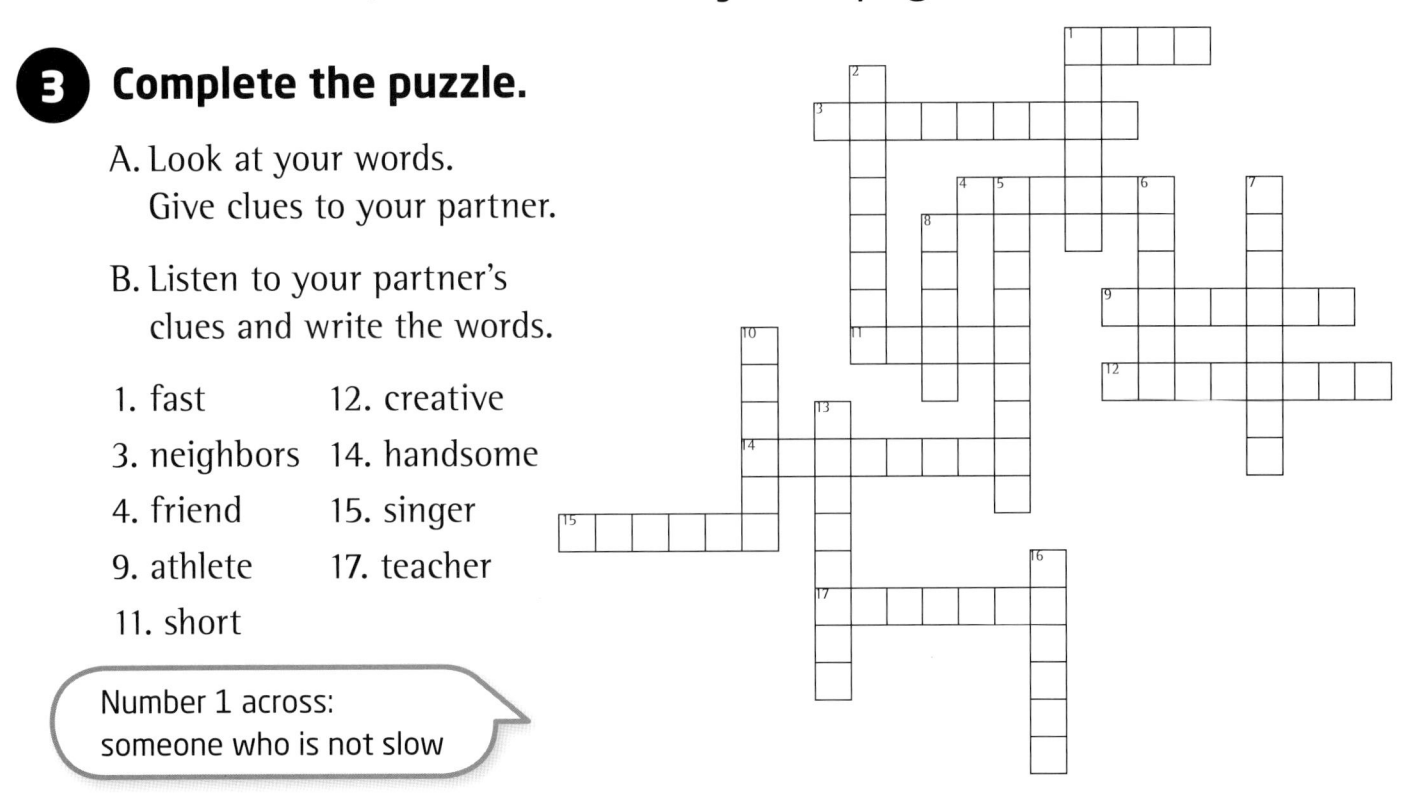

127

Unit 9 Use with Activity 6 on page 125.

6 **Play a game.** In a small group, move around the wheel. When you land on a picture, make a sentence with *the more*. When you land on a number, make a definition with *which* for one of the words in the boxes.

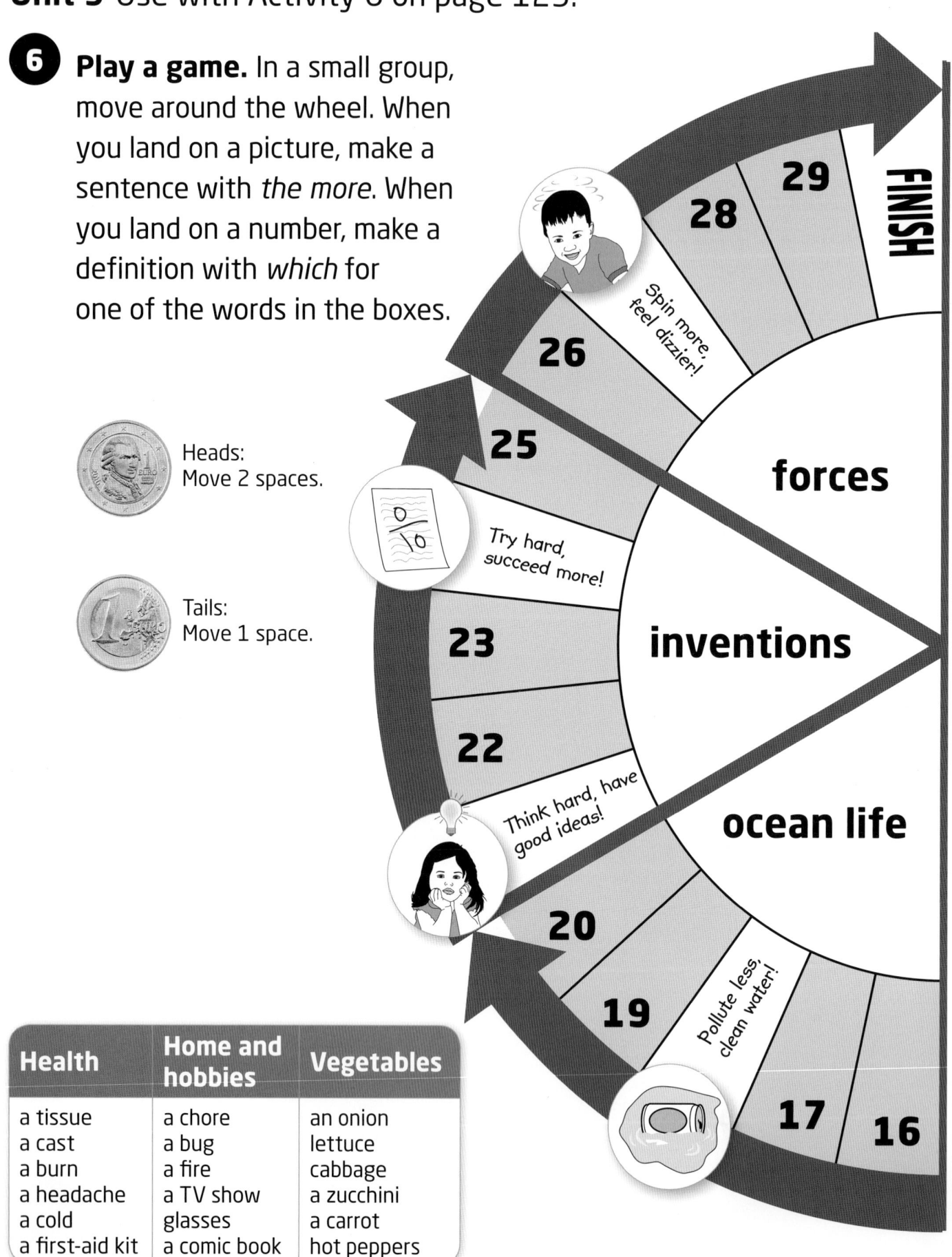

Heads: Move 2 spaces.

Tails: Move 1 space.

Spin more, feel dizzier!

Try hard, succeed more!

Think hard, have good ideas!

Pollute less, clean water!

forces

inventions

ocean life

FINISH

16, 17, 19, 20, 22, 23, 25, 26, 28, 29

Health	Home and hobbies	Vegetables
a tissue	a chore	an onion
a cast	a bug	lettuce
a burn	a fire	cabbage
a headache	a TV show	a zucchini
a cold	glasses	a carrot
a first-aid kit	a comic book	hot peppers

START

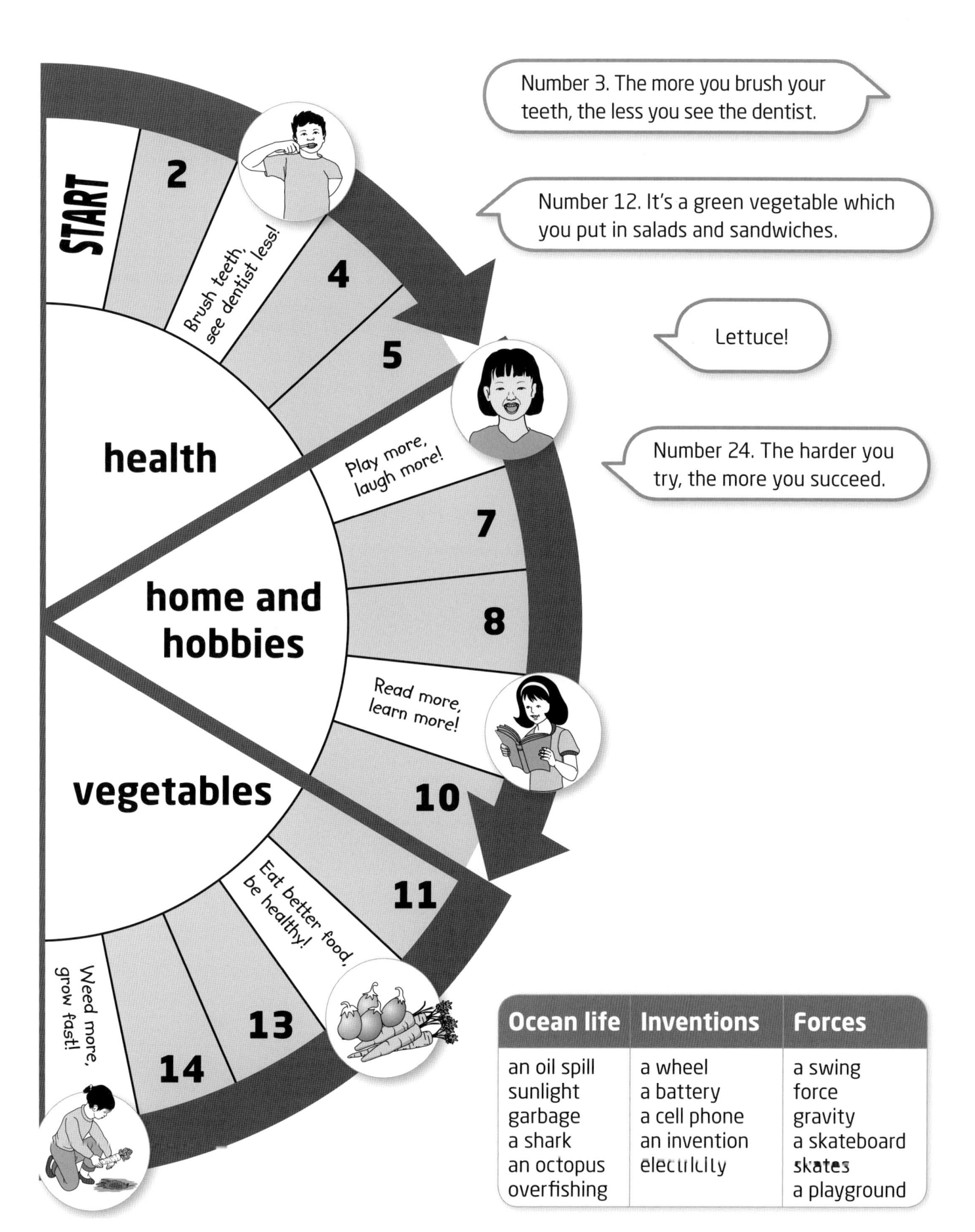

2 — Brush teeth, see dentist less!
4
5
7 — Play more, laugh more!
8
10 — Read more, learn more!
11
13 — Eat better food, be healthy!
14 — Weed more, grow fast!

health

home and hobbies

vegetables

Number 3. The more you brush your teeth, the less you see the dentist.

Number 12. It's a green vegetable which you put in salads and sandwiches.

Lettuce!

Number 24. The harder you try, the more you succeed.

Ocean life	Inventions	Forces
an oil spill	a wheel	a swing
sunlight	a battery	force
garbage	a cell phone	gravity
a shark	an invention	a skateboard
an octopus	electricity	skates
overfishing		a playground

129

Unit 8 Student 2, use with Activity 3 on page 105.

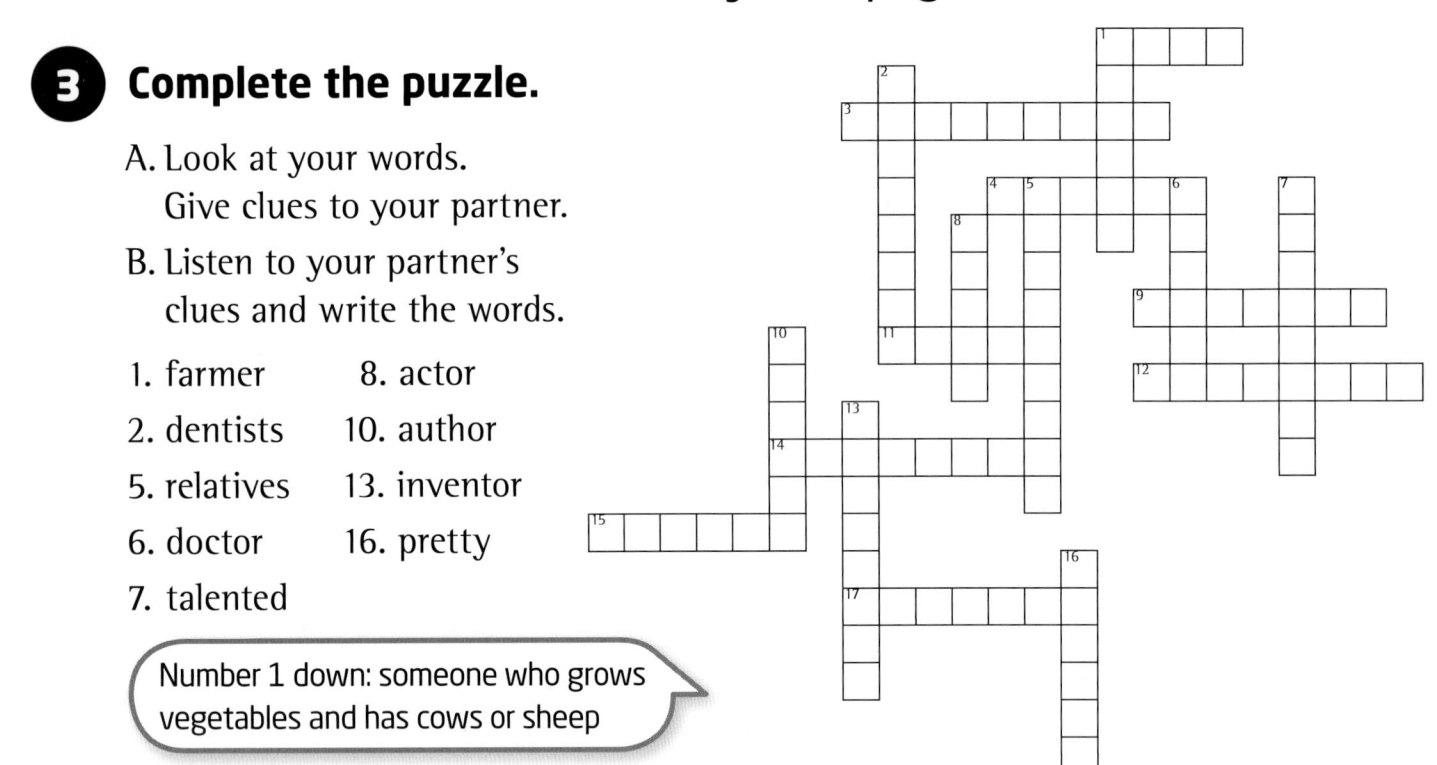

3) Complete the puzzle.

A. Look at your words. Give clues to your partner.

B. Listen to your partner's clues and write the words.

1. farmer
2. dentists
5. relatives
6. doctor
7. talented
8. actor
10. author
13. inventor
16. pretty

> Number 1 down: someone who grows vegetables and has cows or sheep

Unit 6 Cutouts Use with **GRAMMAR 2** Activity 2.

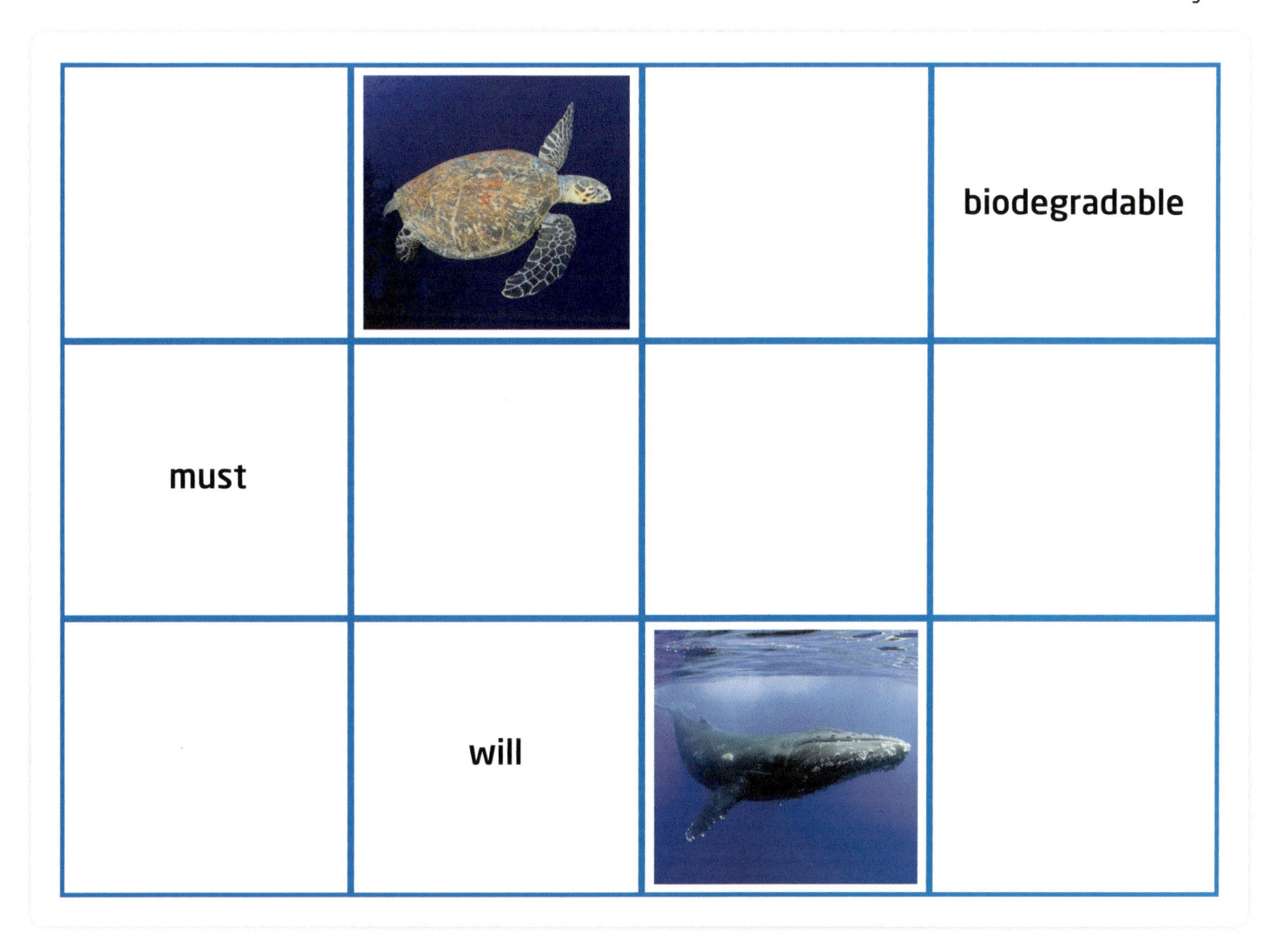

			biodegradable
must			
	will		

131

Unit 7 Cutouts Use with **GRAMMAR 2** Activity 2.

Heads = 1 space   **Tails** = 2 spaces

133

Unit 8 Cutouts Use with **GRAMMAR 2** Activity 2.

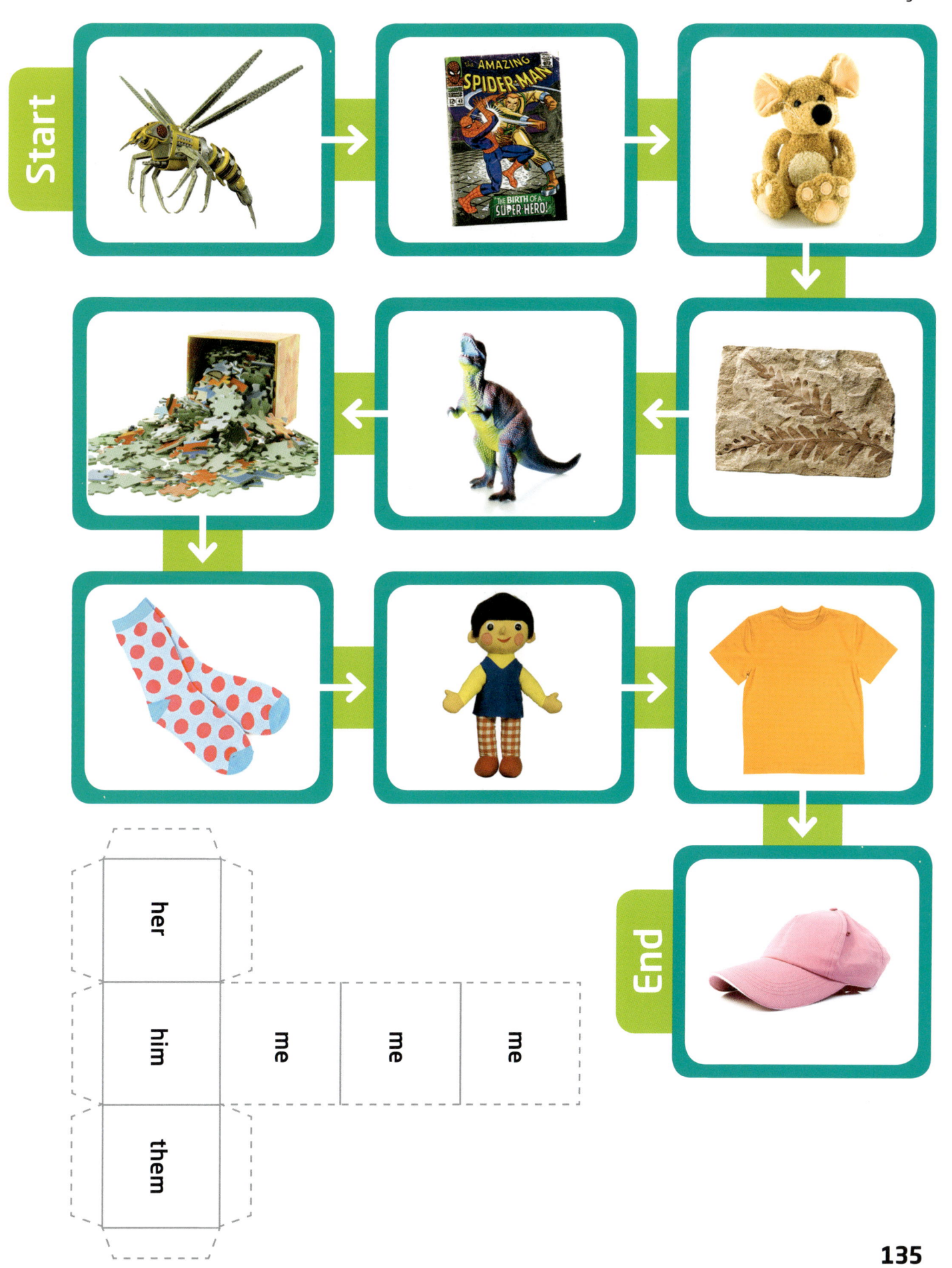

her
him
them
me
me
me

135

Unit 9 Cutouts Use with **GRAMMAR 2** Activity 2.

4	10	12
This is a playground object which goes up and down. What is it?	Act out: "pull"	What is a bicycle? (a machine / wheels and handlebars / which / ride)

14	16	19
Act out: "spin"	What is a skateboard? (a board with wheels / which / move on)	This is a force which pulls you to the Earth. What is it?

24	25	27
Act out: "lose your balance"	What is a cell phone? (a thing / which / use / talk)	This is a game with a ball which you play in the yard. What is it?

30	32	34
Act out: "push"	What is a hobby? (a thing / which / do / free time)	This is a force which happens when two things rub together. What is it?

137

Irregular Verbs

Infinitive	Simple Past	Past Participle	Infinitive	Simple Past	Past Participle
be	was/were	been	light	lit	lit
beat	beat	beaten	lose	lost	lost
become	became	become	make	made	made
begin	began	begun	meet	met	met
bend	bent	bent	pay	paid	paid
bite	bit	bitten	put	put	put
bleed	bled	bled	read	read	read
blow	blew	blown	ride	rode	ridden
break	broke	broken	ring	rang	rung
bring	brought	brought	rise	rose	risen
build	built	built	run	ran	run
buy	bought	bought	say	said	said
catch	caught	caught	see	saw	seen
choose	chose	chosen	sell	sold	sold
come	came	come	send	sent	sent
cost	cost	cost	set	set	set
cut	cut	cut	sew	sewed	sewn
dig	dug	dug	shake	shook	shaken
do	did	done	shine	shone	shone
draw	drew	drawn	show	showed	shown
drink	drank	drunk	shut	shut	shut
drive	drove	driven	sing	sang	sung
eat	ate	eaten	sink	sank	sunk
fall	fell	fallen	sit	sat	sat
feed	fed	fed	sleep	slept	slept
feel	felt	felt	slide	slid	slid
fight	fought	fought	speak	spoke	spoken
find	found	found	spend	spent	spent
fly	flew	flown	spin	spun	spun
forget	forgot	forgotten	stand	stood	stood
forgive	forgave	forgiven	steal	stole	stolen
freeze	froze	frozen	stick	stuck	stuck
get	got	gotten	sting	stung	stung
give	gave	given	stink	stank	stunk
go	went	gone	sweep	swept	swept
grow	grew	grown	swim	swam	swum
hang	hung	hung	swing	swung	swung
have	had	had	take	took	taken
hear	heard	heard	teach	taught	taught
hide	hid	hidden	tear	tore	torn
hit	hit	hit	tell	told	told
hold	held	held	think	thought	thought
hurt	hurt	hurt	throw	threw	thrown
keep	kept	kept	understand	understood	understood
know	knew	known	wake up	woke up	woken up
leave	left	left	wear	wore	worn
lend	lent	lent	win	won	won
let	let	let	write	wrote	written
lie	lay	lain			

My Words

Word	Picture
Word in my language	

Word	Picture
Word in my language	

Word	Picture
Word in my language	

Word	Picture
Word in my language	

Word	Picture
Word in my language	

Word	Picture
Word in my language	

My Words

Word	Picture
Word in my language	

Word	Picture
Word in my language	

Word	Picture
Word in my language	

Word	Picture
Word in my language	

Word	Picture
Word in my language	

Word	Picture
Word in my language	

My Words

Word	Picture
Word in my language	

Word	Picture
Word in my language	

Word	Picture
Word in my language	

Word	Picture
Word in my language	

Word	Picture
Word in my language	

Word	Picture
Word in my language	

My Words

Word	Picture
Word in my language	

Word	Picture
Word in my language	

Word	Picture
Word in my language	

Word	Picture
Word in my language	

Word	Picture
Word in my language	

Word	Picture
Word in my language	

My Words

Word	Picture
Word in my language	

Word	Picture
Word in my language	

Word	Picture
Word in my language	

Word	Picture
Word in my language	

Word	Picture
Word in my language	

Word	Picture
Word in my language	